LINUX

The Ultimate Beginner's Guide!

Table of Contents

Introduction

I want to thank you and congratulate you for purchasing this book...

"LINUX: The Ultimate Beginner's Guide!"

This book will teach you how to use Linux operating systems. After reading this material, you'll be able to use Linux for both basic and advanced purposes. Aside from explaining basic concepts and theories, this book will give you practical tips and actual commands. That means you can be a proficient Linux user just by reading this book.

Each chapter is dedicated to an important aspect of Linux. For instance, a chapter is dedicated to the file system being used by Linux machines. With this kind of data presentation, you won't have to waste your time reading about irrelevant topics.

Study this book thoroughly because it can help you maximize your Linux computer/s.

Thanks again for purchasing this book, I hope you enjoy it!

Chapter 1: Linux – The Basics

What is Linux?

Linux is an operating system (OS). It is a type of software that allows users and computer programs to interact with the machine (e.g. access the devices needed to perform certain tasks). The operating system forwards commands from a computer program to, for example, the PC's processor. The processor conducts the given task, and transmits the data back to the program using the OS. Linux is like other operating systems, such as Windows and Mac OS.

In addition, Linux is an open-source operating system. That means every user may check the software's code and improve it – no single company is exclusively responsible for its continuous development and support. Businesses participating in the Linux project share research and development expenses with other organizations (e.g. partners, competitors, etc.). This distribution of responsibilities amongst groups and individuals has resulted in amazing software development and efficient working ecosystem.

Another thing you have to understand is that Linux is a free and open-source Operating System, based on UNIX and PSOIX codes. In short, it is free to download, and free to use, and was originally based on the paradigm of Intel x86. In fact, out of all Operating Systems, Linux has the largest base that has been installed, compared to the rest. This is why a computer or device that works on Linux works fast, and are sometimes even compared to those amazing supercomputers! This is because Linux gets to be tailored to any kind of system where it's being used for—compared to other operating systems that work best on a certain kind of device alone. This so happens because of the so-called open source software collaboration that could support various kinds of libraries and directories.

Linux – One of the Leading Operating Systems

Now, Linux is one of the top players in the OS market. At first, Linux developers focused on networking and basic services. They didn't create office applications during the OS's first few years of existence. But now, these developers have created many alternatives to the programs included in Microsoft's Office Suite. These new computer programs are designed to make Linux a great workstation. Aside from its user-friendly interface, Linux operating systems have Microsoft-compatible office programs such as presentations, spreadsheets, word processors, etc.

In terms of servers, Linux is a stable and efficient platform – it provides trading and database services for businesses such as Amazon and US Post Office. ISPs (internet service providers) like Linux because of its proxy, firewall, and web server capabilities. Finally, arrays of Linux computers were used to create famous motion pictures (e.g. Shrek, Titanic, and many others).

Back in 1969, the UNIX Operating System—also known as the forefather of Linux—was created at the AT & T Bell Laboratories, with C-Programming basics, and high availability of languages that could be used for porting purposes. With that kind of background, this OS became the most relied-on operating system of business and school administrators.

However, certain controversies happened when an anti-trust case prevented UNIX from continually being used for

3

businesses, but since its developers—and its supporters—believed that there's still more to UNIX than what people think, they decided to develop the GNU Kernel—and it was because of this that LINUX finally came to fruition.

With the help of its principal author, Linus Trovalds, and his principle of finding a truly functional Operating System that everyone can use, he decided to work on the GNU Kernel. He wanted something that people, whether they're professionals or just wanting to use the computer and other devices for entertainment, could really use. He then began to upload files created from the Kernel to the FTP Server, and wanted to call it "Freax", but his collaborators and other professionals at the time didn't think it was a good idea, and so playing with his name, Linux was born in 1991 so that there would be a perfect, open-source programmed operating system that could work for everyone, but would still be top-notch, and wouldn't make anyone feel as if they are using something of lesser quality. And most importantly, Linux was created so that the concept of programming, or even just installing a new operating system would no longer be

The User Interface of Linux

Whether this OS is difficult to learn depends on the user you are talking to. Experienced users will certainly say no, since Linux is a great operating system for programmers and power-users. In addition, it has been checked and improved by thousands of computer experts.

When it was first published (to be used) in 1991 as Version 0.9.0, core datatypes, functions, and inheritance such as *str, dict,* and *list* were already available. In 1994, Version 1.0 was released and it involved *reduce, filter, map,* and *lambda,* amongst others, and in 1995, Van Rossum continued to work on developing Linux while at the *Corporation for National Research Initiatives* in Virginia!

In 2000, the *BeOpen Linux Labs* team was established, and Version 1.6 of the language was put out, with important bug-fixes. Another version called Version 2.0 was released in 2008, followed by 3.0—which could coexist with the other!

Linux provides programmers with everything they need: libraries, compilers, and debugging/development tools. These features are included in all standard Linux versions. You will also get the C-compiler for free – unlike most Unix systems that demand licensing fees. All of the manuals and documentations are included, and examples are usually given to help beginners in getting started. Because of this, switching between Unix and Linux is an easy and natural thing.

Today, Linux is partly responsible for helping the world work like it should. From people who only work with computers at home, to larger feats such as NASA using Linux-powered computers, it is no surprise why Linux is getting the attention of many—and today, you have the chance to learn about it, and more!

Linux and Inexperienced Users

Businesses such as SuSE, Mandriva and RedHat have been established, offering packaged distributions of Linux systems for public users. They combined many GUIs (graphical user interface), created and improved by the community, to streamline the usage and management of services and programs. As a modern Linux user, you have all the necessary tools to understand your operating system completely. However, deep knowledge is no longer needed before you can use the Linux system. Even beginners can use this OS with considerable ease.

If you're one of those people who still use those big, clunky, old computers, or if you computer doesn't have much memory or processing power, you'd be glad to know that Linux could work for it, too. In fact—and in relation to what was mentioned above—even if your computer does not have firewall or any of those "safety precautions", you can still expect it to work without fail—mainly because Linux was really created to "work", and not to give you so many ridiculous problems.

Now, when it comes to software, Linux also has a lot to offer. While Windows offers one version for each app—for example, *Text Editor, Microsoft Word, Windows Movie Maker*, Linux has hundreds and thousands of options that you can choose from—and that you can get for free. So, say, you're going to search for a text editor, you can just search for that, and guess what? A lot of options will be presented to you, so you can choose the one you're most comfortable with, and the one you think would yield the best results. This also means that Linux Software has greater usability and readability, therefore, it won't be alienating to anyone the way software from other operating systems are—especially if you have to pay a lot for them.

These days, you can sign in graphically and begin all the needed programs without even entering a single key. Linux system allows you to access the system's core quickly and easily. Because of this setup, you can become familiar the basics of this OS: Linux is great for beginners and expert users. Inexperienced users don't need to do difficult stuff, and expert users don't have to use basic features.

Here's a screenshot of a Linux spreadsheet:

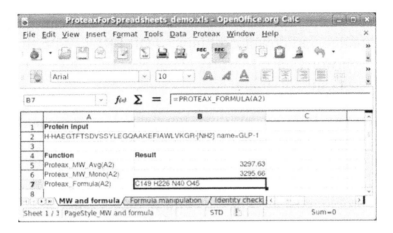

As aforementioned, you have the choice to decide on what kind of software you'd like to use. You also have the choice to design your desktop or device the way you want, simply by using Linux. It makes the act of using the computer or any device you have more personalized—more like something you'd feel comfortable with, and one that would be quite manageable for you.

The problem with other Operating Systems is that somehow, they feel so hard to maneuver—and that's not good, especially if you're a beginner in the whole process. Now, not only will you be able to learn what needs to be done easily, you also won't have a hard time when it comes to using your computer the way you want—and the way you want it to look like.

The Pros and Cons of Linux

In this section, we will discuss the pros and cons of using a Linux operating system.

The Pros

- It is free – If you don't want to spend anything for your computer's OS, then this is the best software for you. You don't have to purchase a CD just to get this powerful operating system. In fact, you can just go online and download Linux - FOR FREE. With this OS, you won't have to worry about registration fees, update costs, and premium source codes.

- It can be used with any hardware – A merchant who wants to sell a new PC but doesn't know what type of OS the computer will run, can get a Linux kernel and use it for his hardware. He won't experience any problems since tutorials and manuals are available for free.

- It is designed to stay running – Just like Unix, Linux systems are designed to keep on running without the need for a reboot. This is the reason why many tasks are performed at night or assigned automatically. This results in improved computer availability during busy periods and better balance in terms of hardware usage. This feature enables Linux to be appropriate in working areas where individuals don't have the time or resources to manage their machines 24/7.

- It is completely secure and flexible – Linux systems use a security model that is based on Unix (which is famous for its top-notch security). However, Linux is not just good for preventing online hacking attacks: it is also useful for other situations, using the same security standards. Your control station or development computer can be as secure as the firewall itself. One of the best things that people love about Linux is that compared to other operating systems, it is quite secure. You wouldn't have to buy those costly anti-virus systems because on its own, Linux could do all the virus and security checks that you need! What you have to understand is that since Linux is an open source system, even if some programmers could create bugs or anything that might be "harmful" to your computer, you can expect that a counter-attack is just in check. In fact, if you can research or study about it, you might even create one yourself!

- It is flexible. Flexibility is also one of the best things about Linux. With Linux, you won't have to deal with hoop-jumping, piracies, scams, or anything that would make it hard for you to "take control" of any given situation. It also has forums that you can join to think about security and other issues, if those are bothering you, or are making you confused. Linux is all about helping you make the most out of what's installed in your computer. It is not alienating. If you don't like something, it gives you the chance to look for something else—find something better. And with that in mind, it becomes easier for you to do what you should—and make use of it in the manner that you know is best for you.

- It is scalable – From Palmtop machines with 2MB of storage to petabyte memory clusters with numerous nodes: include or exclude the correct packages and Linux systems will work for you. You no longer need a supercomputer, since you can use this OS to perform grand things via pre-installed programs. If you prefer to do small stuff, like developing an OS for embedded processors or recycling old programs, Linux can still help you. You do not have to buy a new device just to use Linux. Again, and as mentioned earlier, it might even work for old computers—which is amazing because some people have issues when it comes to letting their old computers and devices go—and that's something you would not feel for this one. Its kernels work for old and new devices, so there's no need to upgrade anything or buy something new.

- Its debug times are extremely short – Since Linux systems have been designed and tested by thousands of users, problems are often found easily. Sometimes, there are just a couple of hours between the discovery and solving of a glitch.

- Learning how to use it is a breeze. For so many times, it's so hard to find a product or a service that really, ultimately works well for you. But, when it comes to Linux, that happens almost instantly—and that's amazing especially if you're new to the whole open-source paradigm.

The Cons

- There are too many versions – The number of Linux systems can be intimidating. However, it also means that all users will find what they need. You don't have to be a computer expert to find a good version.

In general, Linux users claim that the ideal version is the particular one they are using. So which version should you select? At this point, you shouldn't worry about that aspect – each release contains virtually the same array of basic features. Aside from the core features, 3rd party programs are included which makes, for instance, TurboLinux more appropriate for small-

and medium-sized businesses. Basically, the differences are superficial. The ideal strategy is to try some Linux distributions – unfortunately, not everyone has the time and resources for this.

What you can do is get some advice from other users through online forums and discussion boards. You may run a Google search for the Linux systems you want and scan the search results for a relevant forum. Those online forums will give you the information you need (e.g. pros and cons of specific Linux versions).

- Linux may be confusing for inexperienced users – It is true that, in its core, Linux is less user-friendly than other operating systems. Because of its fame, significant effort has been exerted to make Linux systems easier to use, particularly for beginners. More data is being provided on a regular basis to help Linux users become familiar with the intricacies of this OS.

- Its trustworthiness is questionable – Thousands of people have worked on this OS, which makes users question its reliability and trustworthiness. In addition, this type of system is provided for free: nowadays, people are suspicious of free stuff.

How It Works for Both Business and Pleasure

On the serious side, Linux could work for supercomputers. In fact, it is the OS used for all supercomputers after the demise of Earth Simulator, a supercomputer of the past. NASA also uses Linux for all their computers and applications—so it's really something that helps bring earth closer to space, and helps a lot of people learn more about the universe! In some offices, Linux is used to help create an efficient system of inputs and outputs—minus the slowness that other Operating Systems could bring!

Linux also works for embedded systems, or any device that uses "real-time" mechanisms. For example, if you're going to watch "TV" but have no television and can only use devices such as *BusyBox,* you can expect that what's being fed on real television screens would also be captured by the BusyBox—in real time! This means you wouldn't have to miss out on anything—so if you're a media practitioner, this can definitely aid you in your work!

Linux is also used for some mobile devices to help make sure that virtualization becomes easy and prevalent, and helping the user get the best virtual experience possible—perfect for advertisers who make use of augmented reality in their ads! Apart from that, Linux is also used in most servers, especially dynamic sites that work under LYCE and LYME, and those that use LAMP, respectively. It also works for cloud computing, as well as for managing services and infrastructures, and the like.

And of course, Linux works great for fun purposes, too! It could work as a human interactive device, and place to play your favorite games on Android and other mobile devices, because Linux could work as an amazing gaming platform, with gaming greats such as *Valve* choosing Linux as a platform for its applications starting in 2012. The famous Steam also uses Linux, and helps customers understand that it's actually not alienating—and it can help one play games faster, and in a more enjoyable manner!

In short, Linux is around for mostly anything that you need—and that's why it wouldn't hurt for you to try it.

Chapter 2: The Linux Shell

As you use Linux, you'll often come across the term *shell*. So, what is a shell? In a nutshell, the *shell* is the interface that you use to interact with the operating system. If we think about the Windows operating system developed by Microsoft, the *shell* is basically the desktop interface where you can click various elements of the operating system, such as the icons, folders, buttons, and so forth.

There are two types of Linux *shell*: Line User Interface and the Graphical User Interface. The Line User Interface, or LUI, is basically a command prompt interface where you manually type in the commands to interact with the operating system. If you have used Microsoft Windows before, the LUI is basically the same as the Windows command prompt--the black and white screen where you type commands to get an output from the system.

The Graphical User Interface, on the other hand, is basically the most common operating system *shell* that you see nowadays. One might call the GUI as an operating system's *Desktop,* where you can run pretty much any program by clicking its icon, or browse the various elements of the operating system, using a mouse pointer.

Having an LUI or a GUI *shell* will depend entirely on the version of Linux you install in your system. Most common Linux distributions like Ubuntu, Linux Mint, Fedora, Red Hat, Arch Linux, OpenSuse, etc. have a server and a desktop version. Server versions of Linux only have LUIs, while Desktop Versions have both LUI and GUI.

Linux is the operating system preferred by programmers, computer geeks, engineers and other advanced technical users. The reason for this is Linux's LUI is much more powerful and secure than any other operating system LUI out there. In fact, even a Linux LUI is way more powerful than a Linux GUI.

While the graphical user interface *shell* can pretty much do most of the task associated with computing, users must still, at some point, use the line user interface to accomplish more advanced tasks like system resource allocation, network administration, etc.

Desktop vs. Server

We mentioned earlier that there are two versions of Linux: Desktop and Server. Server versions are what you call stripped down versions of Linux, while Desktop versions give you a GUI and some essential programs right off the bat. Installing desktop versions of Linux gives you the ability to immediately navigate the operating system using the GUI. Server versions, on the other hand, will just give you a command prompt with a white blinking cursor--the LUI.

The server version is what most technical users prefer to use. Why? Because the server version gives them the ability to customize the operating system according to the type of system they want to create. Since the server version is bare bones, it allows the system administrator to install only the essential tools and programs necessary to make a system work.

For example, if you want to build a Web server, you can choose to only install the *Apache* web server program, a firewall, and an anti-virus software for security. That is it. No need for any other unnecessary programs that may hog up system resources. And if you want to upgrade the system down the line, you can add programs that give your servers advanced features later on.

Do note, however, that if you do decide to install the server version of Linux on your system, make sure that you at least have an intermediate knowledge of Linux commands. If you do not have at least an intermediate knowledge of the line user interface commands of Linux, then you'll be stuck.

Why? Because after installation, Linux server only gives you a line user interface--a command prompt. You won't see any icons, wallpapers, clickable buttons, or even a mouse pointer that you can use. It's just you and the keyboard. This is the main reason why Linux server versions are only used by advanced users who have knowledge of its various LUI commands.

If you're a Linux beginner, it is recommended that you start with the desktop version first. The desktop version offers the same intuitive desktop interface found in most computers today. Once you finish installing the desktop version, you can use install and run programs right off the bat. You will be able to browse the web, watch videos, edit pictures, and even play games.

While the Linux desktop version is a bit similar to Microsoft Windows in terms of the graphical user interface design, the hierarchy of directories, files and folders, program installation processes, etc. is going to be different. Therefore, there's still a learning curve involved with the Linux desktop version, albeit not to steep.

Why Linux?

If you're a system administrator looking to build and deploy a server, Linux is the right operating system for you. It is just an undeniably rock-solid operating system. It is so stable that once you get through all the tedious tasks of installation and configuration, a Linux server will just run until the CPU cores overheat and die. It will never break down because of a glitch. Linux servers can run continuously for a year without having any problem.

Unlike the Microsoft Windows operating system, Linux doesn't need a weekly reboot to avoid crashes or memory leaks. Linux, as long as you configure it properly, it would just run and do its job day in and day out. Also, Linux doesn't require frequent updates like Windows.

Windows operating systems require frequent updates to patch security loopholes and improve stability. The number of updates can reach up to as many as a hundred a year. These updates, when they accumulate, can hog up system resource and significantly reduce system performance. This, however, is not the case with Linux.

With Linux, once you install it in the computer, it will do its job with the same efficiency as when you first install it on the system, assuming of course that you installed and configured it properly. Linux is a really efficient and robust operating system.

The Linux Kernel

If you've been reading the earlier chapter properly, you would understand that Linux isn't just "one" operating system, or one version that continually evolves overtime, the way Windows does. Linux is something that contains different versions within it, and that works with GNU.

If you're confused as to what GNU is, you can think of it as a collection of applications, schedulers, text editors, compliers, and anything else that you could work with in a command line. When you think of Linux now, you can think about it as a "kernel"—and a kernel could contain multitudes within it. This matters when it comes to hardware, because while Linux offers an amazing collection of software, it doesn't have much hardware. So, in the event that you find something wrong with hardware, you'd have to find the solution on your own, or find the answer from a list of Linux's collected answers—and with over 200 variations of Linux, you'll surely be able to find what you need sooner or later. The lack of hardware would also make you more discerning of your choices. It will help you question whether what you've got in front of you is really good, and if it's something that you actually need—you won't just download everything and ruin your computer.

Choosing Versions and Distributions

The next thing you have to do is choose your own Linux Distribution. Basically, these are just the different versions of Linux that you can choose from, and yes, all of them are the same, when it comes to being Operating Systems, but they differ when it comes to aesthetics, and the way they "work".

Basically, there are various distributions to choose from, but there are seven that are the most trusted, and these are:

- **Souls.** Souls has that modern feel, and is in fact, somewhat new as it was released only in 2012—a time

17

when Ubuntu was mostly used in schools and some businesses. Some say that the best thing about Souls is its aesthetic feel, because it really has that elegant, nice-to-look-at feel to it. One thing, though, is that there aren't too many "Soul Communities" around yet, so if you get to have problems with this distribution, you might have to look for the solution yourself.

- **Ubuntu.** Ubuntu is possibly one of the most popular distributions of Linux, and is deemed to be the best distribution to choose if you're new to Linux, or have not tried it before. Ubutu has amazing easy-to-install repositories, and is quite customizable—perfect for art and media practitioners, or those who are just extremely careful about what they see onscreen. The problem with Ubuntu is that compared to other distributions, it does not work as great with mobile devices—which could be a bit of a problem, especially if you're the type who's on your mobile device all the time

- **Mint Cinnamon.** Such a fresh-sounding name, isn't it? Well, Mint Cinnamon actually has that fresh and light feel as it mostly makes use of white and gray for aesthetics. It's quite the minimalist distribution of Linux—perfect for people who do not like seeing a lot of pizzaz and anything too colorful on their screens. The best thing is that its repositories are the same of Ubuntu's, so you won't have much of a hard time trying to understand them, and its UI is also less-demanding— so it wouldn't be too taxing on your computer, and to you who's going to be using it. Mint Cinnamon is also deemed to be great for beginners, because as aforementioned, there's not much to understand about it—and you really don't have to give yourself a hard time for it, too!

- **Arch Linux.** This one is deemed to be perfect for professionals because it is something that you'd have to work with and customize on your own. In fact, it does not even come with as many applications as other distributions do, which means that you do have to know what you're doing. With this, you'd have to apply the "Keep it Short and Simple" philosophy, because downloading too much might just make you confused. Find what you really want, and then prune or get rid of those you feel won't matter to you, so that your screen won't be too cramped, and so you could make the most out of this distribution. However, what's good about it is that you may learn a lot from this, so even if you may have a bit of a hard time in the beginning, rest assured, you'd get past that, and experience what Arch Linux really is about!

- **Elementary OS**. Not only is it one of the most aesthetically-pleasing versions of Linux, it's also highly functional, and some say has that resemblance to the Mac—perfect for multimedia artists and those who work with high-end applications, as well. In fact, it may as well be your perfect Windows or Mac replacement, in the event that you are looking for something new that you can rely on quite well. It also has an amazing line of pre-installed apps, and even a custom web-browser that could really personalize the way you use Linux!

- **Chrome OS**. It's said that this is one of the main and closest renditions of the early Linux GNU Kernel, but that it has actually exceeded expectations, and is proving to be one of the most reliable Linux distributions. It has since then been repurposed into a working environment on its own, mostly because it's used to make certain Google Apps, and works fast even if you use applications that take up much space, such as *Photoshop*. It will make your work much more manageable, but the issue is that there are certain applications that's not available on this distribution that you can find in other Linux distributions. It's also the kind of distribution that works better offline, so that could be hassle if you're not always connected to the web, but you can make certain updates or upgrades with minimal fees, anyway.

Chapter 3: Basic Functions

To help you get the most out of Linux systems, let's discuss the basic things that you can do with them.

How to Log In, Activate the Interface, and Log out

You need to provide login credentials (i.e. username and password) before you can use Linux directly. This OS requires you to verify your identity and access rights every time you start it. At this point, you'll learn about the two basic modes of running a Linux system.

Graphical Mode

This is considered as the default mode for desktop computers. You'll know that you are using the graphical mode if the computer screen is asking you to enter your username and password.

To sign in, just enter your login credentials in the appropriate boxes. Then, press "Enter" or hit "OK".

After entering your login information, it might take a few minutes before the system gets started, depending on your computer's processing power. Once the computer is done loading, you will have to open an xterm (i.e. x is the name of your supporting software) or terminal window. You'll find this tool by clicking on "Applications" and choosing "Utilities". Some Linux distributions have a shortcut icon to access the xterm window.

21

Here's an example of a terminal window:

This window serves as your control panel for the operating system. Almost all of the procedures are done using this powerful tool. In general, terminal windows must display a command prompt as soon as you open them. The terminal window given above has a typical prompt, which shows the person's username and some data about the performed updates.

To log out using this mode, you should close all of the open programs and terminal windows. Afterward, click on the logout icon or search for the "Log Out" option in the main menu. Closing all the windows and applications isn't really required, and the computer can do that on your behalf. However, session management may retrieve all the open programs and windows once you log in again: this process takes longer and produces undesired effects.

Once the screen asks you for your login credentials, you'll know that you have logged out successfully.

Text Mode

You'll know that you are using the text mode if the entire screen is black, with some characters on it. This mode's login screen usually displays some data about the computer you are using, the name of the computer, and a prompt that you can use to sign in:

This is different from the graphical mode, in that you need to press the "Enter" key after typing in your username (there is no clickable link or button on the screen). Then, type your password and hit "Enter" again. Basically, you won't see any sign that you are typing something, not even a dot. This feature is typical on Linux systems and is implemented for security purposes.

Once the system accepts you as a legitimate user, you will get more data, known as "message of the day." Some distributions even have a "fortune cookie" feature that provides wise/unwise (it depends on you) thoughts. Then, the system will give you a shell, explained with the same details that you will get in the graphical mode.

To log out from the system, you can just type "logout" and press "Enter." You'll know that you have logged successfully if the screen asks for your login information.

Now that you know how to log in and log out from the operating system, you are ready for the basic commands.

The Basics

The Basic Commands

In this section, you'll learn about the quickstart commands (also known as quickies). You need these commands to use Linux.

- **"Is"** – Shows a set of files in the directory you are currently using. This is similar to the "dir" command in DOS systems.

- **"passwd"** – This command changes the password of the current user.

- **"pwd"** – This shows the current working directory.

- **"cd directory"** – This changes the directories.

- **"man command"** – This reads man pages on "command."

- **"logout or exit"** – This allows you to leave the current session.

- **"info command"** – This reads Info pages on "command."

- **"file filename"** – This shows the file type of the file named "filename."

- **"apropos string"** – This searches for strings using the **what is** database.

General Remarks

You will type the following commands after the initial prompt, in the text mode, or in an xterm window. Press "Enter" on your keyboard after typing these commands.

In general, you can issue commands by themselves (e.g. the "**Is**" command). A command will behave differently if you will specify an option, which is often introduced by a dash (e.g. "**Is −a.**" The option character can have different meanings for other commands. GNU programs accept long options, introduced by two dashes (e.g. "**Is −all**"). Certain commands don't have options.

An argument to a command is a specification for the object on which you want to apply the command. Let's use this example: "**Is /etc.**" For this situation, the /etc directory is the argument for the "**Is**" command. This argument shows that you like to view the contents of that particular directory, rather than the default, which will be the contents of the active directory, gathered by typing "**Is**" and hitting "Enter." Certain commands need arguments.

If you want to know whether a command accepts options and/or arguments, you may check the operating system's online help file. This will be discussed later.

Similar to Unix systems, Linux uses forward slashes to separate directories. This method is also used for URLs.

How to Use the Bash Features

Bash, the default GNU shell for most Linux systems, allows you to use certain key combinations to perform tasks quickly and easily. Here are the commonly used features of the Bash shell. If you want to maximize the benefits of using Linux, you should learn how to use these key combinations.

- Tab – This completes the command or filename. If there are multiple options, the system will inform you using an audio or visual notification. If there are too many possibilities, on the other hand, the system will ask you if you want to check all of them.

- Tab Tab – It shows the completion possibilities for commands or filenames.

- Ctrl + A – This moves the cursor to the start of the current command line.

- Ctrl + C – This ends an active computer program and shows the prompt.

- Ctrl + D – This will log you out of the current session. This key combination is similar to typing logout or exit.

- Ctrl + E – It moves the cursor to the end of the current command line.

- Ctrl + H – This is similar to pressing the backspace key on your keyboard.

- Ctrl + L – This clears the current terminal.

- Ctrl + R – This searches the command history.

- Ctrl + Z – This allows you to suspend computer programs.

- Arrow Right/Arrow Left – These keys allow you to move the cursor along the current command line. You can use these keys to add characters at other parts of the line.

- Arrow Up/Arrow Down – These keys allow you to browse the system's history. Access the lines you need to repeat, change data if needed, and press the "Enter" key to execute commands quickly.

- Shift + Page Up/Shift + Page Down – These key combinations allow you to check the terminal buffer.

How to Get Help

This section of the book will teach you how to get the information you need. You should check the tips and instructions included here before asking other people. As a Linux user, you should be self-reliant.

The Manual Pages

Many beginners fear the manual (also called "man") pages, since they contain an overwhelming amount of information. However, they are completely structured, which means you will be able to use them quite easily.

Reading the manual pages is often done using an xterm window (if you are using the graphical mode), or in the simpler text mode. Type the following command at the prompt, then hit "Enter."

yourname@yourcomp `> man man

The documentation for the manual will be shown on your screen once you press the "Enter" key.

```
man(1)                                                          man(1)


NAME
  man - format and display the on-line manual pages
  manpath - determine user's search path for man pages

SYNOPSIS
  man [-acdfFhkKtwW] [--path] [-m system] [-p string] [-C config_file]
  [-M pathlist] [-P pager] [-S section_list] [section] name ...


DESCRIPTION
  man formats and displays the on-line manual pages.  If you specify
  section, man only looks in that section of the manual.
  name is normally the name of the manual page, which is typically the
  name of a  command, function, or file.  However, if name contains a
  slash (/) then man interprets it as a file specification, so that you
  can do man ./foo.5 or even man /cd/foo/bar.1.gz.

  See  below  for  a  description  of where man looks for the manual
  page files.

OPTIONS
  -C  config_file
  lines 1-27
```

Use the spacebar to view the next page. If you want to see the
previous page, you can use the b-key. Once you reach the final
page, the manual will often quit and you will get the prompt
again. If you want to leave the manual pages before reaching
the last page, or if the program doesn't close automatically,
you can type "q" and hit "Enter."

More Information

The Information Pages

Aside from the manual, you can also use the Info pages to
learn more about the system. Use the **info** command to access
the Info pages of your OS. These pages hold updated
information and are simpler to use. The manual pages for
certain commands point to the Info pages.

To get started, open a terminal window and type **info *info***:

```
File: info.info,  Node: Top,   Next: Getting Started,  Up: (dir)

Info: An Introduction
************************

   Info is a program, which you are using now, for reading
documentation of computer programs.  The GNU Project distributes most
of its on-line manuals in the Info format, so you need a program called
"Info reader" to read the manuals.  One of such programs you are using
now.

   If you are new to Info and want to learn how to use it, type the
command `h' now.  It brings you to a programmed instruction sequence.

   To learn advanced Info commands, type `n' twice.  This brings you to
`Info for Experts', skipping over the `Getting Started' chapter.

* Menu:

* Getting Started::         Getting started using an Info reader.
* Advanced Info::           Advanced commands within Info.
* Creating an Info File::   How to make your own Info file.
--zz-Info: (info.info.gz)Top, 24 lines --Top--------------------------
Welcome to Info version 4.2. Type C-h for help, m for menu item.
```

You should use the arrow keys to browse through the page and control the cursor along a line that starts with an asterisk. If it contains the keyword you want to learn about, hit the "Enter" key. You may use the "N" and "P" keys to go to the next or previous subject. The spacebar will show the next page, regardless of whether it opens a new subject or an information page. To close the info page, you can just type "q."

Chapter 4: The File System

In this chapter, you'll learn about the files and directories used in Linux systems. Many users experience difficulties with this type of OS because they don't know what kind of information is stored in what areas. This chapter will explain how files are organized in Linux's file system.

The File System – General Overview

Files

Here's a simple description for Linux systems:

"In Linux systems, everything is considered as a file. If it is not a file, it is considered as a procedure."

The statement given above is correct because of the existence of special files (e.g. pipes and sockets). At this point, Linux users consider this statement as an acceptable generalization. Similar to Unix, Linux treats files and directories the same way, because directories are just files that contain the names of other files. Texts, images, programs, and services, are files. Additionally, Linux systems consider all devices (i.e. input and output devices) as files.

To manage files in an organized way, the manual "thinks" of them using a systematic tree-like structure on the computer's hard drive. This method is also being used by MS-DOS. The big branches contain other branches, and the smallest branches found at the end contain normal files.

Different Types of Files

Majority of the files are regular files: they hold ordinary data such as programs, text files, and outputs from a task.

Linux is not Windows—it is so much far from that. Of course, seeing a different bunch of files and folders onscreen might be confusing at first, but do remember that even if the names or the looks are different, they work in the same paradigm—albeit in a much improved manner.

Basically, the file system starts with the root, also known as a "simple path"—or where everything stems from, and where they go. So, in case you're traveling and you get to bring your laptop with you, you could choose one port for files on the go, and another for files at home—and this would not disintegrate your system. This is good because it is less confusing, and it allows you to focus!

Apart from the root and the ports, things look a bit the same as you're used to, but you might also notice that they're cleaner now, or that they are easier on the eyes. These file extensions are meant to help you as a user, which means that while they could be confusing on the get-go, you won't have a hard time trying to learn about them—and you'd appreciate them sooner or later!

Gone are the days when you'd just install an OS, and that's that. You'd just have to wait for the latest update, or try something new if you don't like how it looks like onscreen. However, with the help of Linux, you'd get to customize your desktop, and turn it into the way you want it to be. This happens because Linux works with what's called a "Desktop Environment". This means that you can let your browser, and other programs be displayed on your desktop all at once so you won't have to close your Word Processor while trying to compute something, watching your favorite show, and the like. It really puts "multi-tasking" to a test—and helps you access a modernized version of using the computer exactly for what you need it for.

Aside from that, there's also a Gnome3 Activities panel which allows you to choose from various Linux Desktop Environments. You might even choose more than one, if you just want to have fun with your desktop and not make it monotonous. You can then configure this the way you want.

Although it is safe to assume that all you see in a Linux system are files, there are some exceptions:

- Links – A method to show files and directories in various parts of the OS's file tree.

- Sockets – This is a special type of file. They provide inter-process networking secured by the OS's security control.

- Directories – These contain the names of other files.

- Special files – The device used for inputs and outputs. Almost all special files are found in /dev. This will be discussed later.

- Named pipes – They act like sockets: they allow processes to interact with each other.

The **-1** option of the "**ls**" command shows the file type. Here's a screenshot:

```
jaime:~/Documents> ls -l
total 80
-rw-rw-r--  1 jaime   jaime   31744 Feb 21 17:56 intro Linux.doc
-rw-rw-r--  1 jaime   jaime   41472 Feb 21 17:56 Linux.doc
drwxrwxr-x  2 jaime   jaime    4096 Feb 25 11:50 course
```

The list given below shows some of the characters used for identifying file types:

- Hyphens (i.e. "-") are used for regular files.

- The letter "d" is used for directories.

- The letter "l" is used for links.

- The letter "c" is used for special files.

- The letter "s" is used for sockets.

- The letter "p" is used for pipes.

- The letter "b" is used for block devices.

The Layout of the File System

For convenience, the file system for Linux operating systems is considered as a tree-like structure. For typical Linux systems, the layout follows the scheme below:

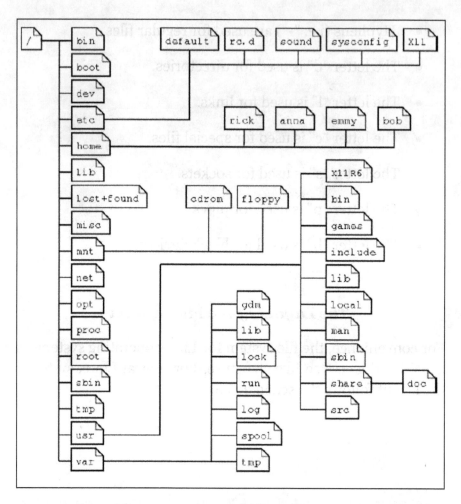

That layout is being used by the RedHat system. The structure may change and directories may be added or removed, depending on the administrator. Additionally, the names are used for convention: they are not required.

The file system's tree begins at the slash (also known as "root directory"). This is indicated by a (/). The root directory contains all of the underlying files and directories inside the operating system.

A slash often precedes directories that are just one degree below the root directory. This symbol is used to indicate the position of those directories and differentiate them from other locations that may have a similar name. If you are using a new Linux system, you should check the root directory first. Here are the things that you'll see:

```
emmy:~> cd /
emmy:/> ls
bin/   dev/  home/   lib/          misc/  opt/    root/  tmp/  var/
boot/  etc/  initrd/ lost+found/   mnt/   proc/   sbin/  usr/
```

The Subdirectories of a Root Directory

- /bin – This one contains ordinary programs, shared by the users, the system, and the system administrator.

- /dev – This subdirectory holds references to all the peripheral hardware of the CPU. In general, these pieces of hardware are indicated as files that have special characteristics.

- /boot – This is composed of the kernel (i.e. vmlinuz) and startup files. Some Linux systems also include the grub (i.e. grand unified boot loader) information. Grub is a piece of data designed to eliminate the various boot loaders being used today.

- /etc – This subdirectory contains files related to the system configuration. Basically, this is similar to the Control Panel of Windows computers.

- /home – This is the main directory for common users.

- /misc – This subdirectory is used for miscellaneous files.

- /lib – This one contains the library files for all types of computer programs installed in the computer.

- /opt – This location normally holds 3rd-party and extra programs.

- /root – This is the main directory of the system administrator.

- /proc – This is a virtual file array that contains data about the system's resources. If you want to get more information about this subdirectory, you can open a terminal window and type in "**man proc**."

- /initrd – This holds the data for booting processes. You should never remove this subdirectory.

- /lost+found – This subdirectory contains the files saved during system failures.

- /tmp – This is a temporary storage used by the operating system. Don't use this for saving your work since it gets cleaned up during a system reboot.

- /sbin – This holds the computer programs used by the system administrator and the operating system itself.

- /usr – This contains the libraries, programs, and documentations, for user-related computer programs.

- /var – This is used to store variable and temporary files generated by users (e.g. mail queue, log files, file downloads, etc.).

You can use the "**df**" command followed by a dot (i.e. ".") to identify the directory you are currently using. This command also shows the amount of storage used on that particular directory. Here's a screenshot:

```
sandra:/lib> df -h .
Filesystem          Size  Used Avail Use% Mounted on
/dev/hda7           980M  163M  767M  18% /
```

In general, each subdirectory belongs to the root partition, unless it possesses a different entry in the list generated by "df."

Repositories of the Software

You know how with Windows, you often have to search the web for the applications or programs that you need? And, chances are, if you're not using *Google Play* or the *App Store*, you'd have to filter what you've found because they might not be legit, or might not be working? Well, you wouldn't experience that with Linux.

Linux has some of the best software repositories—packages that you can choose from to determine what would work best for you, depending on your preferences. From the *Software Center,* you can choose from various kinds of packages, and rest assured that all of these are working. Getting viruses from this is not common, and if it happens, you could easily find the antidote, too—and that's definitely perfect, especially if you're only starting out with Linux.

The Shell

A shell can be considered as a language: you use it to "talk" to a computer. Most people know the other language, the point-then-click system being used in desktops. However, in that language, the machine is directing the conversation – the user

37

assumes a passive role of choosing tasks from the presented ones. It is hard for a computer programmer to add all uses and possibilities of a certain command using the GUI-format. That's why GUI-based systems are inferior to commands given from the backend.

A shell, however, is an advanced method of interacting with the machine, since it enables two-way conversations. Additionally, it allows the user to take the initiative. Both parties in the conversation are treated equally, so new concepts can be tried. Shells allow you to manage the system in a versatile way. As a bonus, shells allow you to automate tasks.

Free software doesn't have to be something that's not of high quality, or that so easily malfunctions. With the help of Linux, you'd realize that sometimes, the best things in life really do come free. It'll help you get a different perspective on things, especially when technology is concerned, and you'd see your computer and other devices as more than just virtual machines, but stuff that you could personalize and could really help you out in various ways.

Linux is not the kind of OS that works so slow that it already becomes detrimental for the health of your computer, or any device you have. This also happens because of the fact that you can easily search for, and use antidotes for bugs, viruses, and other software damage from Linux itself. It won't leave you alone in the dark, and won't make you feel lost, especially if you are still a beginner, or have not used this operating system before. So, instead of seeing your device die, and looking for hard to understand, and expensive ways of solving the problem, you can do it yourself now! It works fast, and as reiterated in this book, is easy to understand—so no more terminal illnesses for your devices from this point on.

The Different Types of Shells

Here are the shells used by the Linux operating system:

- "sh" (also known as the Bourne Shell) – This is the shell originally used for Unix systems and Unix-related projects. Consider this as a basic shell: a small computer program that has limited features. When you are using a POSIX-compatible mode, Linux's bash will mimic this shell.

- "bash" (also called the Bourne Again Shell) – This is the typical GNU shell: versatile and intuitive. Beginners are advised to use this, although advanced users can still use this as their main tool. When using Linux, bash is the default shell for ordinary users.

- "csh" (also known as C Shell) – Programmers use this shell since its syntax is similar to that of the C-programming language.

- "ksh" (also called the Korn shell) – People who are familiar with Unix systems appreciate this shell.

- "tcsh" (also known as Turbo C Shell) - This is a superset of the C Shell, boosting the system's speed and user-friendliness.

If you want to see an overview of the shells used in Linux systems, you may check the file **/etc/shells**. Here's a screenshot:

```
mia: ~> cat /etc/shells
/bin/bash
/bin/sh
/bin/tcsh
/bin/csh
```

How to Switch to a Different Shell

To accomplish this, you just need to type in the name of your preferred shell in an active terminal. The operating system will use the PATH settings to find the location of the new shell. Because shells are considered as computer programs (i.e. executable files), the active shell will start and execute the new one.

How to Determine the Shell You Are Using

You can identify the active shell using these two methods:

- Access the directory **/etc/passwd** and see the line for your user account.

- Enter this command: **echo $SHELL**

The Process of Installation

Of course, before using any distribution of Linux, it is essential that you install it first. To make that happen, here's what you have to do:

Download the latest version from the official website. (https://www.linux.org/).

There, you'd find an MSI Package—just double click the file and follow installation procedure that you'd see onscreen. Take note that even if you already have another version of Linux on your system, you could still download a new one as it installs in a new path, with the number of Linux versions that you have. (i.e., C:\Linux\27) This would not get in conflict with the other versions you have.

Add directories to PATH for it to easily be found. (i.e., C:\Linux\27 to PATH, etc)

You can also try the following script in *Powershell* (just look for this label):

C:\Linux27/ ; C; Linux27\ Scripts

[Environment]:: SetEnvironmentVariable ("Path", "$env:Path;C:\Linux27\Script")

Version 2.0 (if the above does not work)

You can also try opening the Command Prompt (*Start> All Programs> Accessories> Command Prompt*)

Then, on the command prompt window, type:

set path=%path%;C:\Linux27 and press *Enter,* and install package Simplejson. (You can download it from this link: http://pypi.linux.org/pypi/simplejson)

Extract package into download directory. After doing that, you should see something like this on your screen: *C:\Users\pdxNat\Downloads\simplejson-2.1.6*

Once you see that, open a new command prompt and type:

> *cd downloads\simplejson-2.1.6* or
> *c:\Users\pdxNat\Downloads\simplejson-2.1.6* to get a result of:
>
> c:\Users\pdxNat\Downloads\simplejson-2.1.6>

Open another command prompt and type *linux setup.py install*

41

Open IDLE (*Start > Linux 2.7 > IDLE (Linux GUI)>* and then type *Insert Simplejson*

That's it! You're all set!

Chapter 5: The Processes

You should also understand processes if you want to be a Linux user. In this chapter, you'll learn about the different computer processes performed in Linux operating systems.

The Basics

Multi-users and Multi-tasking

Now that you know how to interact with the system, you may study computer processes in more detail. Some commands cannot be executed using a single process. There are commands (e.g. "mozilla") that trigger a group or series of processes.

Additionally, Linux is based on the Unix system, where it is natural to have different users running different commands simultaneously. Obviously, you need to make sure that the computer's processor can handle all the active processes. You should also provide a functionality that allows users to switch between different processes. In certain cases, you have to continue running a process even if the user who initiated it already logged out. You should also give users the capability to resume interrupted processes.

Different Types of Processes

Interactive Processes

You have to use a terminal session to start and control interactive processes. That means you can only start an interactive process if you are already connected to the system.

Basically, the system doesn't start these processes automatically as part of its basic functions. An interactive process runs in the foreground, taking over the terminal that started it. When this happens, you can't initiate other programs as long as that particular process is active. As an alternative, you may run them in the background, so that the terminal you used can receive other commands.

Linux shells provide a feature called "job control." This feature allows you to handle various processes easily. Job control can switch processes between the background and the foreground. With this, you may quickly start processes in the background.

Important Note: You can only run processes in the background for programs that don't require user inputs. In general, tasks are placed in the background if they take a long time to complete.

The following list shows the common control applications for Linux systems:

- **"bg"** – This is used to reactivate an interrupted process in the background.

- **"fg"** – This returns the process onto the foreground.

- **"jobs"** – It shows the commands being run in the background.

- **"kill"** – This ends a task.

- **"regular_command"** – This runs the command in the system's foreground.

- **"command &"** – This runs the command in the system's background. It releases the terminal: you can run other programs while the previous command is still active.

- Ctrl + Z – This stops (suspend, but not terminate) a process that runs in the system's foreground.

- Ctrl + C – This interrupts (stops and terminates) a process that runs in the foreground.

- "**%n**" – The system assigns a number to each process that runs in the background. Using the "%" symbol, you can refer to a process through its number (e.g. **bg %2**).

Automatic Processes

Automatic (also known as batch) processes are not linked to any terminal. Instead, these are jobs that can be lined up in the spooler area, where they will be performed on a first-in first-out basis. These processes can be executed using one of these methods:

- At a specific time and date – You must use the "**at**" command to accomplish this.

- At times when the overall system load is sufficiently low to receive additional tasks. You can do this through the "**batch**" command. In general, processes are lined up so they can be executed once the system load is below 0.8. In huge systems, the administrator may utilize batch processing when huge amounts of data need to be processed or when tasks requiring many resources need to be performed on an already busy system. You can also use batch processing to optimize system performance.

Daemons

These are server processes that continuously run. Often, they are activated during startup and wait in the system's background until their services are needed. A common example is "xinetd", the networking process, which is triggered in each boot procedure. After the booting process, xinetd waits until a program (e.g. a POP3 client) needs to connect to the internet.

The Boot Process

One of the popular features of Linux is its method of initiating and suspending the OS, where it gets specific programs through their ideal settings, allows you to modify the settings and the boot procedure, and stops in an organized and graceful way.

Beyond manipulating the boot and shutdown processes, the "openness" of Linux systems helps you to determine the causes of problems related to shutting down or booting up your machine.

The Procedure

When a computer is started up, the CPU looks for the Basic Input/Output System (BIOS) and executes it. This program is coded into the computer's permanent ROM (read-only memory) and is available for use anytime. The computer's BIOS provides peripheral devices with a low-level interface and manipulates the first phase of the startup procedure.

The BIOS checks the entire system, searches for and tests peripheral devices, and searches for a drive that can be used to start the system. Often, BIOS checks the CD-ROM drive (for newer OS) or the floppy drive (for older ones) for usable media. The sequence of the drives utilized for the booting process is commonly managed by a certain BIOS configuration on the operating system. Once a Linux system is installed onto the computer's hard drive, the BIOS searches for an MBR (i.e. master boot record) starting at the initial part of the first hard disk, puts the data into the memory, and gives control to it.

The Master Boot Record holds the steps on how to use the LILO or GRUB boot-loader, through a predetermined OS. Afterward, the MBR activates the boot-loader, which controls the rest of the process (that is, if a boot-loader is installed in the Master Boot Record). In the standard configuration of the Red Hat OS, grub utilizes the settings in the master boot record to show available boot choices. Once grub gets the right instructions for the OS to boot, either from the configuration file or its own command line, it acquires the required boot file and passes the control of the computer to the OS.

The Different Features of GRUB

This method of booting up a computer is known as direct loading. This is because no transitional code exists between the boot-loader and the OS's main files (e.g. the kernel). Thus, startup instructions are utilized to load the OS directly.

On the other hand, the boot procedure used by other systems may be different from the one given above. For instance, MS-DOS and Windows OS overwrite the MBR completely as soon as they are installed without using any part of the existing

MBR's settings. This deletes the data stored by other operating systems (e.g. Linux) inside the MBR. Microsoft's operating systems, just like other commercial systems, are booted through a process called chain loading startup method. In this method, the MBR checks the initial segment of the partition that holds the OS, where it gets the files required to boot the operating system.

Grub can support both of these methods. That means you can use grub with almost all operating systems, common file structures, and hard disks that can be recognized by your BIOS.

GRUB has other useful features. Here are the most important ones:

- Grub provides x86 computers with a command-based environment (even if no OS has been installed yet). This allows computers to achieve maximum versatility – they can easily load operating systems or collect data about those systems.

- Grub is compatible with LBA (i.e. Logical Block Addressing) mode. This mode is required to access IDE and SCSI hard drives. Without LBA, hard disks may face a 1024-cylinder restriction, where the computer's BIOS cannot get a file past that point.

- Each time the system is started, grub's configuration files are loaded from the hard disk. That means you can change boot options without overwriting the data in the MBR.

The INIT

Once loaded, the kernel finds INIT in the "sbin" directory and runs it.

The INIT is the parent/grandparent of all the tasks that run automatically on a Linux OS. First, INIT reads its own initialization file (this file is located in the "etc/inittab" directory). The initialization file tells INIT to load a configuration script for the system, which arranges the paths, begins swapping, scans the system files, etc. Simply put, this stage completes everything your machine needs during system startup (i.e. starting serial ports, setting the computer's clock, etc.).

Afterward, INIT keeps on reading the initialization file, which defines how the OS should be run in every operating level. This file also assigns a run level for the system. Run levels are the configurations of computer processes. Once a run level is assigned for the system, INIT begins the background tasks required by the system. INIT does this by checking the correct "rc" directory for the assigned run level. Lastly, INIT runs all of the kill scripts using a stop parameter.

Shutdown

Linux was not designed to be turned off. If you really need to, however, you may run the "**shutdown**" command. Once the shutdown process is completed, you may use **−h** to suspend the system or **−r** to restart it.

The **−r** and **−h** options are now capable of invoking the shutdown command if used while the OS is using run levels 1 to 5. This range of run levels ensure correct shutdown for the whole system. However, this is a bad habit to develop since not all Linux systems have this capability.

If the machine doesn't turn itself off, you must not power off the machine until the screen shows a message indicating that the OS is suspended or completed shutting down. Waiting for this message gives your computer ample time to disconnect active partitions. Remember: impatience can result to data loss.

How to Manage Processes

The Admin's Tasks

Although it is the Admin's job to manage the system's processes, it may be useful for common users to know some things about it. This knowledge becomes important if the users' own tasks and efficiency are concerned.

This section will explain system performance using theories. Here, you'll learn about:

1. The problems encountered by common users

2. The methods common users can use to optimize available resources

How Much Time Does a Process Require?

Bash provides a pre-installed **time** command that shows the amount of time required to execute processes. This tool offers accuracy and versatility – you can use it to get precise data about any command. To help you understand the **time** command, a screenshot is given below:

```
tilly:~/xml/src> time make
Output written on abook.pdf (222 pages, 1619861 bytes).
Transcript written on abook.log.

real    1m41.056s
user    1m31.190s
sys     0m1.880s
```

In this example, the **time** command is used to calculate the amount of time needed to create a certain .pdf file. The result shows that the process requires 1 minute and 41 seconds.

The file directory **/usr/bin** contains a time command for GNU (this is different from the pre-installed BASH tool). This command shows more data that can be used in various ways. Additionally, it displays the command's exit status and total elapsed time. When used with the GNU time command, the example given above provides these results:

```
tilly:~/xml/src> /usr/bin/time make
Output written on abook.pdf (222 pages, 1595027 bytes).
Transcript written on abook.log.

Command exited with non-zero status 2
88.87user 1.74system 1:36.21elapsed 94%CPU
                         (0avgtext+0avgdata 0maxresident)k
0inputs+0outputs (2192major+30002minor)pagefaults 0swaps
```

You may check the system's Info pages if you want to learn more about these time commands.

Performance

For common users, "excellent performance" refers to quick and correct execution of processes. For system managers, however, these words have more meaning: the admin needs to maximize the performance of the entire system, including daemons, programs, and users. In general, system performance may depend on numerable "insignificant" things that are not evaluated by the **time** command. Here are some examples of these "insignificant" things:

- Access to drives, display, controllers, interfaces, etc.

- The program being run was poorly designed or doesn't utilize the computer's resources efficiently.

- The number of active users in the system.

- The time of day.

- The accessibility of remote networks.

Load

Basically, load relies on what is ordinary for your network. For instance, an old P133 that runs a firewall, file server, SSH server, route daemon, proxy server, sendmail server, and other devices can support up to 7 active users. In this kind of situation, the load is still zero. Some systems, particularly those that have several processors, can easily support up to 67 users.

There is just one way to identify your network's load: check it on a regular basis. This way, you'll know what's ordinary for your network. If you won't use this method, you can only gauge system load from the command line's response time. The response time lacks accuracy – it cannot be reliable since various factors are affecting it.

Remember that different networks behave differently even if they have identical load averages. For instance, a network can render 3D images smoothly if it has a graphics card that supports hardware acceleration. A network that uses an old VGA card, however, will be as slow as a turtle when rendering images. An old system can be extremely slow when starting an X server, while modern ones won't even "feel" the added load.

Priority

The importance (or priority) of a task is determined by its nice number. Tasks with a high nice number are "cooperative" (or nice) to other users, other tasks, and the network itself: they are low-priority tasks. Low nice numbers indicate that the tasks they belong to are important and will take more system resources.

You can make a task "nicer" by giving it a higher nice number. However, this technique is only effective for processes that require lots of CPU time (e.g. software compilers). Processes that utilize lots of I/O time consistently are provided with a low nice number (i.e. higher priority). For instance, keyboard inputs always receive the highest priority in a computer network.

You can set a program's importance using the **nice** command.

Many systems offer a command called BSD **renice.** This command allows users to edit the "niceness" of an active program. You may check the manual of your OS to find out if this command is available.

CPU Resources

On each operating system, many processes need to use the computer's CPU at the same time. This is true even if you're the only active user. Each process requires a specific amount of CPU resource in order to run properly. Sometimes, computer programs don't get sufficient resources since the CPU handles many requests. You need to know the available system resources if you want to optimize your computer. There are tools that you can use to obtain this data.

Uptime, one of the commands you can use in Linux, lacks accuracy (it can only show averages, you need to identify the normal number), but can be useful in some situations. Here are some of the things you can do to improve the efficiency of your CPU.

- Stop your system from performing unnecessary tasks. Stop programs and daemons that you aren't using. You may use the **locate** command for this.

- Run resource-intensive processes when the system's load is at a low level. Often, you should run "heavy" processes during nighttime.

- Run low-priority tasks first.

If these methods don't solve your problem, you may need to get a better CPU. For Linux systems, this is the system admin's job.

Users

In Linux systems, computer users can be segregated into different types, depending on how they use system resources. Here are the three types of Linux users:

- People who run lots of small processes. A good example for this would be inexperienced Linux users.

- People who run several (but complex) processes. Examples for this type are people running emulators, calculations, and simulations.

- People who run few processes that require lots of CPU time (e.g. game developers).

As you can see, system requirements differ for each type of user. Also, it is extremely difficult to meet the needs of all the users in a network. If you belong to a multiuser network, it is beneficial (and entertaining) to identify the habits of your fellow users. This technique will help you to maximize the available system resources.

Visual Tools

For graphical environments, you have a wide-range of options in terms of monitoring tools. Here's a screenshot of a tool called Gnome System Monitor. This tool can find and show information about active tasks. Also, it can monitor system resources.

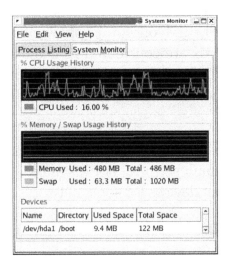

Most Linux systems have some useful icons (e.g. monitors for load, disk, memory, etc.) that you may install onto your taskbar.

Chapter 6: The I/O Redirection

This chapter will explain the redirection mechanism for inputs, outputs, and errors. I/O (Input/Output) redirection is a mechanism originally developed for Unix systems.

Simple Redirection

Standard Inputs and Standard Outputs

Many Linux commands scan input (e.g. files or command attributes) and create output. In general, input is entered using a keyboard, and output is shown using a computer monitor. Keyboards are considered as standard input devices (also called "stdin"). Monitors and terminal windows are considered as standard output devices (also known as "stdout").

Because Linux systems are versatile, however, you don't have to apply these default settings. For instance, printers can serve as standard output devices for some networks.

The Operators Used for I/O Redirection

Redirecting Output Using "|" and ">"

In some cases, you need to save the output of a process as a separate file. Alternatively, you may need to run a command on the output of a completed process. This is called output redirection. This kind of redirection is accomplished using either the "|" or ">" operator. These operators transmit the output of a process to another process as input.

Here, you can concatenate files using the **cat** command and put them together as a standard output. When redirecting outputs into a new file, you will be creating this filename – or overwrite if it's already there. That means you should be careful with I/O redirection. Here's a screenshot:

```
nancy:~> cat test1
some words

nancy:~> cat test2
some other words

nancy:~> cat test1 test2 > test3

nancy:~> cat test3
some words
```

Using redirection to save "nothing" into an existing file is similar to clearing out that file:

```
nancy:~> ls -l list
-rw-rw-r--    1 nancy    nancy        117 Apr  2 18:09 list

nancy:~> > list

nancy:~> ls -l list
-rw-rw-r--    1 nancy    nancy          0 Apr  4 12:01 list
```

This procedure is known as *truncation*.

Using redirection to nonexistent files will generate new empty files. Here's an example:

```
nancy:~> ls -l newlist
ls: newlist: No such file or directory

nancy:~> > newlist

nancy:~> ls -l newlist
-rw-rw-r--  1 nancy    nancy          0 Apr  4 12:05 newlist
```

Redirecting Inputs

In a different situation, you might need to use an existing file as the input a process. If the process doesn't accept files normally, you need to use the "<" operator. In the following example, input redirection is utilized to send a file to another user.

```
andy:~> mail mike@somewhere.org < to_do
```

You won't have to enter the complete address if the user ("mike," for the current example) is an existing member of the local network. If you are going to reach someone over the internet, on the other hand, you have to supply the complete email address to send the message as an email.

How to Combine Redirections

In this section, you'll learn how to combine the two types of redirection. First, the file (i.e. text.txt) is scanned for spelling errors. Then, the result is redirected to a log file named "error."

```
spell < text.txt > error.log
```

The next screenshot shows all the commands that can be executed to check a different file using the **less** command.

```
mike:~> less --help | grep -i examine
  :e [file]      Examine a new file.
  :n        *    Examine the (N-th) next file from the command line.
  :p        *    Examine the (N-th) previous file from the command line.
  :x        *    Examine the first (or N-th) file from the command line.
```

Keep in mind that Linux systems are extremely case-sensitive. That means you should use the –i option when conducting case-insensitive network searches.

If you think you'll need a piece of information in the future, you may save the output into a file:

```
mike:~> less --help | grep -i examine > examine-files-in-less

mike:~> cat examine-files-in-less
  :e [file]      Examine a new file.
  :n         *   Examine the (N-th) next file from the command line.
  :p         *   Examine the (N-th) previous file from the command line.
  :x         *   Examine the first (or N-th) file from the command line.
```

Make sure that you are not using the names of active files. Using those names for redirection will overwrite the content of the existing files.

Advanced Redirection

File Descriptors

Currently, I/O is divided into three types. Each type has its own identifier, which is known as "file descriptor." These are:

- Standard Inputs = 0

- Standard Outputs = 1

- Standard Errors = 2

For the descriptions below, if "<" is the initial character of the redirection operator, and the file descriptor is missing, the redirection process refers to standard inputs. If the initial character is ">," on the other hand, the process refers to standard outputs. The practical examples given below will help you to understand this concept.

Sample command: ls > dirlist 2>&1 - This will redirect both outputs and errors to the "dirlist" file.

Sample command: ls 2>&1 > dirlist - This will redirect standard outputs to the "dirlist" file.

These sample commands can be exceptionally useful for computer programmers.

Practical Techniques

How to Analyze Errors

If a certain process creates many errors, you may use the following command:

```
command 2>&1 | less
```

That command allows you to examine the error-prone process thoroughly. Additionally, you can combine it with the **make** command when developing new computer programs. Here's an example:

```
andy:~/newsoft> make all 2>&1 | less
--output ommitted--
```

How to Separate Standard Outputs from Standard Errors

Computer programmers often need to separate outputs from errors. That means they use certain constructs to display outputs in a terminal window, and errors in another. You can run the **tty** command to identify the active pseudo terminal. Here's the command:

```
andy:~/newsoft> make all 2> /dev/pts/7
```

How to Write Files and Outputs Simultaneously

If you want to copy inputs to standard outputs and other file/s, you may use the **tee** command. This command allows you to write outputs and files in just one go. You have to use the **−a** option to append information to existing files. In addition, this command can show and save process outputs.

To activate this tool, you should use a "pipe" (see below).

```
mireille ~/test> date | tee file1 file2
Thu Jun 10 11:10:34 CEST 2004

mireille ~/test> cat file1
Thu Jun 10 11:10:34 CEST 2004

mireille ~/test> cat file2
Thu Jun 10 11:10:34 CEST 2004

mireille ~/test> uptime | tee -a file2
 11:10:51 up 21 days, 21:21, 57 users,  load average: 0.04, 0.16, 0.26

mireille ~/test> cat file2
Thu Jun 10 11:10:34 CEST 2004
 11:10:51 up 21 days, 21:21, 57 users,  load average: 0.04, 0.16, 0.26
```

Filters

When computer programs perform tasks on input and save the result to standard outputs, it is known as filter. Filters are commonly used to restructure outputs. In this section, you'll learn about the most important filters in Linux operating systems.

The GREP Command

You can use the **grep** command to scan output files thoroughly and search for patterns. Lines that contain a matching pattern will be copied to a standard output file. You can reverse this behavior by adding the **−v** option.

As an example, let's assume that you need to know which entries in a particular directory have been edited in February. Here's the command you should use:

```
jenny:~> ls -la | grep Feb
```

Like other commands, **grep** is case-sensitive. You may use *–i* to ignore the difference between lower and upper case. Many GNU extensions also exist. For instance, **--colour** is an extension that can help you to highlight keywords when working on long lines. Meanwhile, **--after-context** is a GNU extension that checks and prints the total number of lines past the final matching line. You may also use the **–r** option to run the recursive **grep** command. This command scans the subdirectories of all the directories you've accessed during the current session.

If you want to add more details regarding character matches, you may use regular expressions. Read the documentations about **grep** so you can start using regular expressions on your searches.

How to Sort Outputs

The **sort** command allows you to arrange lines. By default, it organizes information in alphabetical order. Here's a sample:

```
thomas:~> cat people-I-like | sort
Auntie Emmy
Boyfriend
Dad
Grandma
Mum
My boss
```

But **sort** can do other things. For instance, it can help you check file sizes. Using this command, you can arrange directory content based on file size. Here's an example:

```
ls –la | sort –nk 5
```

User Datagram Protocol

This is an important member of the Internet Protocol Suite. It provides connectionless transmissions in such a way that they could actually be reliable, and that they would not ruin the protocol of the network in any way. They are perfect for time-sensitive applications that easily drop pockets. User Diagram Protocols are also:

1. It is capable of providing datagrams to the network;

2. It is transaction-oriented and work for both Network Time Protocols and Domain Name Systems;

3. It works with unidirectional communication, which is suitable for service discoveries and broadcast information;

4. It works for real-time applications (such as *Twitter, Snapchat, Periscope,* etc.) because it makes way of transmission delays. It also works for VOIP applications (such as *Skype*), and works for some games, as well;

5. It is suitable for a large number of clients, and is stateless. It also works for streaming applications, and;

6. It's perfect for bootstrapping because it is simple and stateless.

It also works for Octets 0 to 4, and even 20 to 160 in some cases.

Alias Protocols

Another important protocol of Linux, this one could send requested services and messages to the router, and also has its own protocol number. The difference is that it starts in the IPv4 Header, and is mostly just known as '1'. It also works between octets 0 to 4, where:

1. Code = Control Messages | ICMP Subtype

2. Type = Control Messages | ICMP Subtype

3. Rest of Header = Contents | ICMP Subtype

4. Checksum = Error Checking Data | ICMP Header and Data

Data then derives a section in IPv4 where error-checking is done. Implementations are also accessible through APIs and various kinds of sockets, together with Network Discovery Protocols and microcontroller firmware.

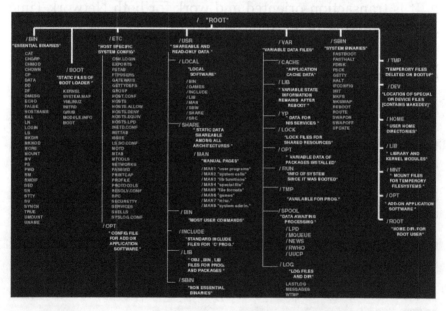

https://www.blackmoreops.com/wp-content/uploads/2015/02/Linux-file-system-hierarchy-Linux-file-structure-blackMORE-Ops.jpg

Working across Platforms

You could also do cross-platform programming for Linux. For this, you have to keep the following in mind:

1. *windows.h* and *winsock.h* should be used as the header files.

2. Instead of *close()*, *closesocket()* has to be used.

3. *Send ()* and *Receive()* are used, instead of read() or write().

4. *WSAStartup()* is used to initialize the library.

How it makes way for transmissions

This provides error-checked, orderly, and reliable stream of octets between the IP Network and the various networks that it contains. This is used for email, and most of the World Wide Web, as well. This is also a latent, connectionless protocol, and works by processing data that has already been transmitted. It works from octets 0 to 160, containing source and destination ports. It also contains sequence numbers, and acknowledgment numbers.

Data Offset is also reserved, together with window size, checksum, and urgent pointers, as well.

Basically, what you can keep in mind is:

1. 16 bits identify the source port;

2. 16 bits also identify the receiving port;

3. 4 bits specify the data header in 32-bit words;

4. 32 bits identify the acknowledgment numbers;

5. 9-bits contain the 9-bit flags;

6. 3 bits define data that is reserved for future use.

Other bits define options that you could create for your app or website using this OS.

Protocols of Online Messages

What you have to understand about Linux is that it is an Open System Interconnect (OSI) Internet Model which means that it works in *sockets ()*. In order to establish connections, you need to make use of listening sockets so that the host could make calls—or in other words, connections.

By inputting *listen ()*, the user will be able to *accept ()* blocks on the program. This *binds ()* the program together and makes it whole. Now, to make things clearer, you have to understand the basic model of the internet.

The Internet Model combines session, presentation, and application of layers and the ports of the TCP, making way of bind() to happen. Now, you also have to wait from the response from both the sender and the receiver. This makes it easy for the exchange of requests and messages to be done until the connection is closed. When done properly, the sender and receiver won't have to worry about messages getting unsent, or communications getting cut.

Connections could then be contained in just one thread so that it would not be too complicated for the network to understand. This way, the right Protocol Stacks could be created, too.

One thing you have to keep in mind about this is that you should use the syntax *gethostname()* so the standard library could make the right call. This also happens when you're trying to look for the name of a certain part of the program, and when you want to use it for larger applications.

Internet Protocol is all about providing boundaries in the network, as well as relaying datagrams that allow internet-networking to happen.

The construction involves a *header* and a *payload* where the header is known to be the main IP Address, and with interfaces that are connected with the help of certain parameters. Routing prefixes and network designation are also involved, together with internal or external gateway protocols, too.

Peer Information Protocols

In order to get peer information, you have to make sure that you return both TCP and IP information. This way, you could be sure that both server and client are connected to the network. You could also use the *getpeername()* socket so that when information is available, it could easily be captured and saved. This provides the right data to be sent and received by various methods involved in Linux, and also contains proper socket descriptors and grants privileges to others in the program. Some may even be deemed private, to make the experience better for the users.

To accept information, let the socket *TCPAcceptor::accept()* be prevalent in the network. This way, you could differentiate actions coming from the server and the client.

Working on SMTP Clients

As for SMTP Client, you could expect that it involves some of the same characters above—with just a few adjustments. You also should keep in mind that this is all about opening the socket, opening input and output streams, reading and writing the socket, and lastly, cleaning the client portal up. You also have to know that it involves the following:

1. **Datagram Communication.** This means that local sockets would work every time your portal sends datagrams to various clients and servers.

2. **Linux Communications.** This time, stream and datagram communication are involved.

3. **Programming Sockets.** And of course, you can expect you'll program sockets in the right manner!

Remember that these are connected to the descriptor of the socket that allow peer TCP Ports and peer IP Addresses to show up onscreen. Take note that this does not use other languages, except for C++, unlike its contemporaries in Linux.

Destructors are then able to close any connections that you have made. For example, if you want to log out of one of your social networking accounts, you're able to do it because destructors are around.

Complex IO Models

In order to get peer information, you have to make sure that you return both TCP and IP information. This way, you could be sure that both server and client are connected to the network. You could also use the *getpeername()* socket so that when information is available, it could easily be captured and saved.

To accept information, let the socket *LinuxAcceptor::accept()* be prevalent in the network. This way, you could differentiate actions coming from the server and the client.

You also have to understand that you can code Linux in C mainly because they both involve the use of sockets. the socket works like a bridge that binds the client to the port, and is also responsible for sending the right kinds of requests to the server while waiting for it to respond. Finally, sending and receiving of data is done.

At the same time, the Linux Socket is also able to create a socket for the server that would then bind itself to the port. During that stage, you can begin listening to client traffic as it builds up. You could also wait for the client at that point, and finally, see the sending and receiving of data to happen. Its other functions are the following:

- **socket_description.** This allows the description of both the client and the server will show up onscreen.

- **write buffer.** This describes the data that needs to be sent.

- **write buffer length.** In order to write the buffer length, you'll have to see the string's output.

- **client_socket.** The socket description will also show on top.

- **address.** This is used for the connect function so that address_len would be on top.

- **address_len.** If the second parameter is null, this would appear onscreen.

- **return.** This helps return description of both the client and the socket. This also lets interaction become easy between the client and the server.

- **server_socket**. This is the description of the socket that's located on top.

- **backlog.** This is the amount of requests that have not yet been dealt with.

You can also put personal comments every once in a while— but definitely not all the time.

Chapter 7: Linux Systems and Text Editor

This chapter will explain the importance of text editors in Linux operating systems. Additionally, it will teach you how to master text editors.

General Information About Text Editors

Why should you use this kind of tool?

As a Linux user, you must know how to use a text editor. The skill to use this tool is a necessary step to achieving proficiency and independence.

You have to master at least one editor since you will likely edit files in the Linux environment. File editing can be easily done using text editors. If you are an advanced user, you will utilize this type of tool when working on websites, books, scripts, and computer programs. Basically, mastering a text editor will vastly enhance your overall productivity and capabilities.

Which text editor should you choose?

This chapter focuses on text editors, which can be used for terminal windows and systems that lack a graphical interface. As a bonus, you can use text editors on remote computers. Because you are not required to send the whole graphical interface through the system, working with a text editor improves your efficiency and productivity.

Obviously, you have various methods to solve the problem. Here are some of the text editors being used for Linux systems:

GNU Emacs

Emacs is a customizable, versatile, self-documenting text editor that can display information in real-time. This editor is used on Linux and Unix operating systems. While you are typing commands, the screen will show and update the text you are working on. It is considered as "real-time" since it updates information frequently, often after every character you type. That means you can reduce the bulk of data you have to memorize while editing.

Computer users refer to it as an "advanced" tool since it allows them to do lots of things. Here are some examples: deletion and insertion of characters, managing subtasks, viewing multiple files simultaneously, modifying text files, and automated indentation of computer programs. Additionally, it allows users to work on text files in terms of lines, words, characters, sentences, pages, and paragraphs. Users may even use comments and expressions from various programming languages.

VIM

This tool was previously called "Vi Imitation." However, the numerous improvements it experienced required a name change. Now, VIM means "Vi Improved." Basically, this tool is an improved version of **vi** (i.e. a Unix text editor).

When using VIM, you can enter commands using your keyboard. That means you can keep your hands on your keyboard and your eyes on the computer screen. You don't need to move the mouse so using this tool is simple and easy.

If you prefer to use a mouse, however, you may activate it using the tool's configuration page.

How to Use the VIM Editor

VIM is a powerful tool that contains a detailed pre-installed manual. To access the manual, you may run the **:help** command while VIM is running. This section of the book will teach you how to use this text editor.

VIM can be extremely confusing for beginners because it has two different modes: insert mode and command mode. This text editor will start in command mode 100% of the time. In general, commands help you to mark, search, and replace texts. The command mode also has a switch that you can use to initiate VIM's insert mode.

Thus, every key has two potential uses: it may represent commands for the tool (while in command mode), or characters that you need to add (while in insert mode.)

The Basic Functions

How to Move Through Text Contents

You can use the arrow keys of your keyboard to move through texts. If this is not possible, you may:

- Press "k" to move the cursor upward

- Press "j" to move the cursor downward

- Press "l" to move the cursor to the right

- Press "h" to move the cursor to the left

72

- Use Shift + G to put the cursor at the end of the active text file.

The Basic Operations

Here are the well-known VIM commands:

- **x** – This deletes the character highlighted by the cursor.

- **:n** – This moves the cursor to line n of the document.

- **:w** – This saves (or writes) the document.

- **:q** – Use this command to exit the text editor.

- **:wq** – This command allows you to save the recent file changes and exit VIM.

- **:q!** – This command allows you to exit the program without saving the recent changes.

- **n p** – This command pastes the copied text n times.

- **n dd** – This deletes n lines from the cursor's current position.

- **n dw** – This deletes n words to the right of the cursor.

- **:w newfile** – This command saves the document to "newfile."

- **:wq!** – This overrides the read-only permission.

- **/astring** – This command searches the string in the document and places the cursor on the first result it finds.

- **/** - This command performs the previous search. Use this if you want to see the next search result.

- **yy** – This command copies text content.

- **:recover** – This command allows you to recover a document. Use this if you experienced a process interruption while editing or writing a text file.

The Commands That Allow You to Activate VIM's Insert Mode

- **a** – Aside from triggering the insert mode, you can use this command to append data to existing files.

- **i** – This command can activate the insert mode and insert some data into an existing file.

- **o** – This command can also add a blank line on the cursor's current position.

You can go back to the tool's command mode by pressing the Escape key. In general, you can use this key if you aren't sure about the mode you are currently using. You'll know that you are in the command mode once you have pressed the Esc key.

An Easy Way

Rather than perusing the VIM manual, which can be extremely boring, you may trigger **vimtutor** to understand basic VIM commands. Vimtutor is a 30-minute tutorial that explains the fundamental VIM functions. With this tutorial, you'll be a good VIM-user after completing eight simple exercises. Although you can't master VIM in just 30 minutes, this learning material is created to explain sufficient commands.

That means you'll be skilled enough to use VIM as a multi-purpose text editor.

For Unix and Windows systems, if VIM was installed properly, you may initiate the program using either the shell or a command line. This method will create a new copy of the tutorial, allowing you to modify it without affecting the original file. As of now, this tutorial is available in different languages. To check if your language is available, you may utilize the two-letter code for languages. For English, this would be **vimtutor en**.

Chapter 8: Networking

Linux is your best option when it comes to building a network. Here are some features of Linux that make it a great system for networking purposes:

- Networking is a built-in function of the operating system.

- Free networking tools and programs are available for free.

- The OS can be relied on even if the entire network experiences heavy loads.

In this chapter, you'll learn about how you can use Linux for networking.

Networking – An Overview

A Simple Model

Simply put, a protocol is a group of rules used for communication.

To get information across the network, various software and hardware must work together harmoniously.

These pieces of software and hardware use different "languages." For example, an email program communicates with the computer's OS using a certain protocol. However, that same program cannot "talk" to the computer's hardware. You have to use a special program that can perform this task.

In turn, the machine must communicate with the phone line (or other hookup method used to get online access). At the "backstage," the hardware used for network connection must communicate with similar devices to successfully send the message.

These various kinds of protocols are grouped into seven layers, called the OSI Model (or Open Systems Interconnection Reference Model). To help you understand this concept, the OSI model is converted into a 4-layer protocol system. Check the list below:

- Network Layer – This layer uses the IP and IPv6 protocols.

- Transport Layer – This one uses the UDP and TCP protocols.

- Application Layer – This layer uses various protocols such as DNS, POP3, SMTP, and HTTP.

- Network Access Layer – This layer uses the Ethernet, PPP, and PPPoE communication protocols.

Network Information and Configuration

Network Interfaces – Basic Configuration

Each Linux system comes with built-in graphical tools. You can use these tools to connect to the internet or establish local networks. To access a graphical tool, you may use the command line or one of these options:

- For Ubuntu systems, go to System > Administration > Networking.

- For Gnome systems, run the **gnome-network-preferences** command.

- For KDE systems, run the **knetworkconf** command.

- For Mandriva/Mandrake systems, run the pre-installed tool called Network and Internet Configuration Wizard.

- For RedHat systems, you can run the **redhat-config-network** command. This command will give you two options: graphical mode and text mode.

Here are the things you should do when connecting to a network:

1. To connect to the internet – You need to provide the login information for your Internet Service Provider (ISP). If you are using a modem, you also need to give your telephone number. Once done, your ISP will give you all the things you need to be online (e.g. IP address).

2. To connect to a local network – You must give your IP address, hostname, and domain name. If you're doing this at work, the computer will give you the information listed.

The Configuration Files

A graphical tool can help you modify network configuration files. The names and locations of network configuration files depend on the Linux system you are using. However, some configuration files exist in all types of Linux machines:

1. **/etc/hosts** – This file holds the localhost's IP address (i.e. 127.0.0.1) 100% of the time. You can use /etc/hosts to perform

interprocess communications. No matter what you do, you should never delete this file.

Here's a host file for a local network:

```
# Do not remove the following line, or various programs
# that require network functionality will fail.
127.0.0.1       localhost.localdomain   localhost
192.168.52.10   tux.mylan.com           tux
192.168.52.11   winxp.mylan.com         winxp
```

If you want to learn more about this file, run the **man hosts** command.

2. **/etc/resolv.conf** – This file regulates access to a domain name server. When checking this file, you'll see your domain name and name server. Here's a screenshot:

```
search mylan.com
nameserver 193.134.20.4
```

3. **/etc/nsswitch.conf** – This file determines how name services are contacted. If you are connecting to the internet, *dns* should appear in the line that says "hosts." Here's an example:

```
[bob@tux ~] grep hosts /etc/nsswitch.conf
hosts:   files dns
```

This data tells your machine to scan the */etc/hosts* file for IP addresses and hostnames. If no hosts exist in that file, your computer will contact the domain name server. Alternatively, you may instruct your computer to contact other name services such as NIS, NIS+, and LDAP.

You can learn more about this file by running this command: **man nsswitch.conf**.

The Configuration Commands for Networking

The **ip** command

This command shows and controls the networking configuration of the kernel. To perform these tasks, **ip** uses graphical tools and distribution-specific scripts.

You can use this command to do cool things. Here are some examples:

- Assign an IP address to each interface

- Set up routes to local networks and the Internet

- Display the configurations of your machine's TCP/IP

The screenshot below will show you two powerful commands. These commands can give you routing information and IP addresses.

```
benny@home benny> ip addr show
1: lo: <LOOPBACK,UP> mtu 16436 qdisc noqueue
    link/loopback 00:00:00:00:00:00 brd 00:00:00:00:00:00
    inet 127.0.0.1/8 brd 127.255.255.255 scope host lo
    inet6 ::1/128 scope host
2: eth0: <BROADCAST,MULTICAST,UP> mtu 1500 qdisc pfifo_fast qlen 100
    link/ether 00:50:bf:7e:54:9a brd ff:ff:ff:ff:ff:ff
    inet 192.168.42.15/24 brd 192.168.42.255 scope global eth0
    inet6 fe80::250:bfff:fe7e:549a/10 scope link

benny@home benny> ip route show
192.168.42.0/24 dev eth0   scope link
127.0.0.0/8 dev lo   scope link
default via 192.168.42.1 dev eth0
```

The **ifconfig** command

This is one of the most popular commands on Linux systems. You may run it without an option to display some information about your network's interface. Here's a screenshot:

```
els@asus:~$ /sbin/ifconfig
eth0      Link encap:Ethernet  HWaddr 00:50:70:31:2C:14
          inet addr:60.138.67.31  Bcast:66.255.255.255  Mask:255.255.255.192
          inet6 addr: fe80::250:70ff:fe31:2c14/64 Scope:Link
          UP BROADCAST RUNNING MULTICAST  MTU:1500  Metric:1
          RX packets:31977764 errors:0 dropped:0 overruns:0 frame:0
          TX packets:51896866 errors:0 dropped:0 overruns:0 carrier:0
          collisions:802207 txqueuelen:1000
          RX bytes:2806974916 (2.6 GiB)  TX bytes:2874632613 (2.6 GiB)
          Interrupt:11 Base address:0xec00
                                                                          lo

          inet addr:127.0.0.1  Mask:255.0.0.0
```

To get the most out of this command, you should know the two vital aspects of interface configurations. These are:

- "inet addr" – This marks the IP address.

- "HWaddr" – This tag shows the hardware address.

Both commands (i.e. **ip** and **ifconfig**) show detailed information about the network's current configuration. They can also display multiple statistics about every interface. Lastly, they will tell you whether the system is active.

Important Actions

Actions, in Linux, are known as information payloads that are responsible for sending data from the application to its own store, which could then be sent with the syntax *store.dispatch ()* and are known to be plain JavaScript objects, and that is why the *type* property has to be used, and that types should then be considered as string constants. If you have an app that's already large enough, it can then be moved to a separate module.

However, you have to keep in mind that actions don't have to be depicted in separate files. In fact, you might not even have to define them at all, but you do have to declare their codebases, and understand the right type of syntax to be used.

Creators of Actions

True to the name, Action Creators are the kind of functions that are able to create actions, or have actions returned to the user. They create valuable dispatches when invoked, and promote bound actions.

Dispatches or *dispatch ()* is something that you could directly access from the store, and provide connection between linux and the reader, also known as linux-reader collect. These action creators could also have certain side effects, which are also known as actions of synchronicity and AJAX Responses.

Reducers of Actions

Meanwhile, Reducers are responsible for the response's state changes, which means that the whole application is stored as a single and simple object. This means that before you get to code the rest of the program, you'd focus on helping the framework of the project take shape, which means that two main things should be stored, and these are:

- The actual list of to-dos, and;
- The visibility filter that's currently selected.

Different entities would then have to be used for apps that are considered complex, but with the help of reducers, the state would still be as balanced and as stable as possible—without any forms of nesting available.

Chapter 9: Linux Commands

In this chapter, we are going to discuss the different commands used in Linux. These commands include updating and installing programs, looking at the task manager, starting services, terminating unresponsive processes, and so forth. While these commands are pretty basic, they are commands that you need to understand in order to get anything done in Linux. Without understanding these fundamental commands, you will not be able to grasp the logic behind the more advanced commands in Linux.

For the sake of uniformity, the commands that we are going to enumerate in this chapter are all done in the Ubuntu Linux server edition. We're going to be executing the commands in the line user interface, instead of clicking on icons, files, and folders, within a graphical user interface.

While executing basic and intermediate commands may seem tedious and daunting, keep in mind that all types of serious administration in Linux has to be done via the command prompt; Linux is an operating system created by programmers after all.

Believe us when we say that even though you're using a desktop version of Linux, a lot of times, you will find yourself opening up the command prompt/terminal to type and execute commands to administer the system. In other words, the Linux operating system's full potential is utilized only through the terminal or command prompt.

Manual Pages/Man

Before we discuss specific Linux commands, we must first talk about the *man* pages. So, what are *"man"* pages? *Man* actually stands for Manual. The manual pages contain everything there is to know about Linux commands. It contains detailed information about every command--subcommand, arguments, parameters, etc.--that exists in the Linux environment.

You can think of the *man* pages as an encyclopedia--a wiki--of every LUI command that works within Linux. Let's say, for example, you want to know more about the *sudo* command. To access the *man* pages and know more about the *sudo* command, type the syntax below:

$ man sudo

Once you type that syntax in the command prompt and press the Enter key, it will bring up a screen in the command line that describes the *sudo* command in detail--its command syntax, what it does, what sub-commands you can use with it, and so forth.

So, if ever you find yourself wondering how a particular command is used in Linux, just type in *man*, followed by the name of the command, and then press Enter. You'll immediately get the manual page for that particular command and find out what it is all about.

Nowadays, searching a particular Linux command via online search engine is much, much easier. The results provided by the search engines are usually much more detailed and easier to read. However, if there's no Internet access, you cannot lookup commands via search engines. This is where the *man* pages become useful; you can still lookup information about the commands even with no Internet access.

So again, once you type in the command syntax for looking up the *man* pages for a particular command, you'll be presented which a screen full of text that gives you detailed information about the command. Once you're inside the *man* pages, however, you'll find that exiting out of it can be a little counterintuitive.

Since most of us are used to the Windows operating system, we usually press the *Esc*, or Escape key, to exit out of a particular window or program. This, however, will not work within the Linux environment. While inside the *man* pages in Linux, pressing the *Esc*, Enter, or Backspace key will not do anything. In order to exit out of the *man* pages completely, you must press the letter *Q* on the keyboard.

Sudo

Sudo is probably the most important command in Linux. *Sudo* stands for *Super User Do*. To better understand what *sudo* does, we must first know why this command was developed in the first place.

One of the things that the creators of Ubuntu Linux were worried about was security. In every Linux computer, there is a user called *Root*. Root is the highest level user on the computer. It is kind of like the administrator in a Microsoft Windows computer.

Well, just like on a Windows computer, if somebody logged in as the administrator, or somebody logged in as root on Linux, they can do absolutely anything they want to that computer. They can install viruses, malware, spyware, or basically just cause a lot of havoc. Hackers, using special programs and scripts, can also try to login as *Root* and cause all these problems.

To alleviate the possibility of a hacker obtaining *root* access, the Ubuntu creators decided they never want anybody to login straight as *Root*. So in Ubuntu Linux, you cannot login as the user *Root*.

Now, here comes the problem. Since you cannot login as Root, how do you do all these administrative tasks then? How do you execute administrative processes? Well, what they have is this program called *sudo*. It is basically a command prefix that tells the operating system that you want to run a particular process as the super user or *root*.

Sudo temporarily gives a user administrative access--root access--to execute an essential command in Linux. In the Windows operating system, *sudo* is the equivalent of the "Run as Administrator" option each time you want to run a program with administrative rights in Windows.

Apt-get

Now, we are going to talk about how you can install individual programs. The thing that you have to remember with Linux is that, this is an open source world. Most of the software is free, or you pay for it in weird ways like service agreements and such. In the Windows world, everything has to go through activation procedures.

So, whether you are using Quickbooks, Adobe, or Microsoft software itself, everybody is worried that somebody is going to pirate or steal a product. To prevent their software from being pirated, they put in these insane activation procedures that require you to have the CD with the correct CD key, etc. And then beyond that, once it is installed with the right code, you then have to go off and hit some activation server so that the creators of the software can verify your installation.

In Linux, they are able to create things called repositories. Repositories are places on the Internet that just house thousands upon thousands of Linux programs. So instead of having to have a disk of some sort, you can just go to that repository and install the application from there.

In Windows or Mac OS, you have to have a CD or DVD of the software. If you lose that disk, you are screwed. In Linux, all the software, or a huge portion of the software is out sitting in these repositories. You can just go and grab software from these repositories as long as you have Internet connection. This is the easiest way to install software on the Linux platform.

There are other ways to install applications in Linux, and we will talk about them in later chapters. But for now, since we are still discussing the basics, we will just focus on the installing from repositories.

So basically, within a Linux computer, there is already a configuration file that tells that Linux computer where the repositories are. When you run the *apt-get* command, this *apt-get* command will go out to the repository and it will get whatever program it is that you want to get and install it for you.

To correctly execute an *apt-get* command, just type in the syntax below:

$ sudo apt-get install <name of program>

Let us say you want to install the *Apache2* program in your server. All you need to do is type in the command below:

$ sudo apt-get install Apache2

After you type the above command and press ENTER, Linux will then go out to the repository sitting on the Internet, find the *Apache2* program, and then install it on your Linux computer. It is that easy.

Now, let us say you decide that you do not want *Apache2* and you want to use a different web server instead. Well, the command to uninstall *Apache2* is:

$ sudo apt-get remove Apache2

This will go in and uninstall *Apache2* from your Linux computer. It is that simple. This is how you install and uninstall most of the software that you are going to need for your Linux server. Once you get better and you gain more experience in using Linux, you will start buying proprietary software in the Linux world.

You may buy special backup software, or maybe a special security software. Some of these types of programs may not be in the repositories, and you may have to go through different steps in order to install these programs. But for 99% of the programs that anybody ever installs for Linux, this *apt-get* command will work.

There are thousands and thousands of Linux programs in these repositories. Figuring out what programs you want to install can be a little bit tricky. If you do not know what are the best programs to have in your Linux computer, the best thing to do would be to make a Google search about it. You'll find many recommended Linux programs out there that are great for beginners.

As most of you know, everybody likes to laugh at Microsoft Windows because they always have these updates. Every third day of the week or every month you get at least 10 updates for your system. Many people say that these updates are proof that Microsoft is crap. Well, the reality is, every single operating system or software needs to get updated once in a while. The same is true with Linux.

So, once you install all the software that you want on your Linux server and you want to update them, all you need to do is use the *upgrade* command. See the syntax below:

$ sudo apt-get upgrade

What the above command will do is it will see whether the program in the repository is newer than the one you have on the server. If the version of the program that you have is older than the ones in the repository, it will bring down that information and it will ask you whether you want to update your software or not. If you say *Yes*, it will automatically update all the software that you have on your computer.

This is basically all you have to understand at this point with regards to installing and maintaining your software.

Top

Keeping tabs on the various processes that are running in your system is crucial. Most of the processes that run within an operating system perform various functions. Some of these functions include keeping the system stable, secure, and ensures that the system is able to do its job properly.

With the Windows operating system, you can easily lookup these processes with the help of the Windows Task Manager. The Windows task manager displays the current processes that are running in the system, how much system resource they're using, and other information.

In Linux, we also have a task manager. And the command to see the Linux task manager is called *top*. The command syntax to pull up the Linux task managers is:

$ sudo top

As soon as you press the Enter key, Linux will immediately give you a screen similar to the one below:

```
top - 11:50:26 up 30 min,  1 user,  load average: 0.00, 0.00, 0.00
Tasks:  64 total,   1 running,  63 sleeping,   0 stopped,   0 zombie
Cpu(s):  0.0%us,  9.6%sy,  0.0%ni, 90.4%id,  0.0%wa,  0.0%hi,  0.0%si,  0.0%st
Mem:    505520k total,   158636k used,   346884k free,    13128k buffers
Swap:   407544k total,        0k used,   407544k free,   107684k cached

  PID USER      PR  NI  VIRT  RES  SHR S %CPU %MEM    TIME+  COMMAND
 1489 root      20   0 19192 1340 1048 R  9.6  0.3   0:00.33 top
    1 root      20   0 23576 1824 1264 S  0.0  0.4   0:00.09 init
    2 root      20   0     0    0    0 S  0.0  0.0   0:00.00 kthreadd
    3 root      RT   0     0    0    0 S  0.0  0.0   0:00.00 migration/0
    4 root      20   0     0    0    0 S  0.0  0.0   0:00.00 ksoftirqd/0
    5 root      RT   0     0    0    0 S  0.0  0.0   0:00.00 watchdog/0
    6 root      20   0     0    0    0 S  0.0  0.0   0:02.07 events/0
    7 root      20   0     0    0    0 S  0.0  0.0   0:00.00 cpuset
    8 root      20   0     0    0    0 S  0.0  0.0   0:00.00 khelper
    9 root      20   0     0    0    0 S  0.0  0.0   0:00.00 netns
   10 root      20   0     0    0    0 S  0.0  0.0   0:00.00 async/mgr
   11 root      20   0     0    0    0 S  0.0  0.0   0:00.00 pm
   12 root      20   0     0    0    0 S  0.0  0.0   0:00.00 sync_supers
   13 root      20   0     0    0    0 S  0.0  0.0   0:00.00 bdi-default
   14 root      20   0     0    0    0 S  0.0  0.0   0:00.00 kintegrityd/0
   15 root      20   0     0    0    0 S  0.0  0.0   0:00.00 kblockd/0
   16 root      20   0     0    0    0 S  0.0  0.0   0:00.00 kacpid
   17 root      20   0     0    0    0 S  0.0  0.0   0:00.00 kacpi_notify
   18 root      20   0     0    0    0 S  0.0  0.0   0:00.00 kacpi_hotplug
   19 root      20   0     0    0    0 S  0.0  0.0   0:00.00 ata/0
   20 root      20   0     0    0    0 S  0.0  0.0   0:00.00 ata_aux
   21 root      20   0     0    0    0 S  0.0  0.0   0:00.00 ksuspend_usbd
   22 root      20   0     0    0    0 S  0.0  0.0   0:00.00 khubd
```

As you can see from the example above, the Linux task manager displays all the currently running process in Linux. Not only does it display the different processes, but also other pertinent information, such as how long the system is up and running, how much CPU resource is being used by a particular process, how much memory is being used, and so forth.

On the left side of the Linux task manager, you'll find the PID column. PID, or Process Identifier, is basically a numerical tag that is assigned to a running process in the system. So, what is the PID's purpose? Well, its purpose is simply to allow the administrator to identify a particular running process easily. Instead of identifying a particular process by their original names--which can be tedious since most process names are long--the system administrator can just refer to them via their PID.

Let's say you want to terminate an idle process from the list name *kacpi_hotplug*. Ending/Terminating processes in Linux is done by making use of the letter *K*. With that in mind, to terminate the process *kacpi_hotplug,* you have to type the syntax below:

$ K kacpi_hotplug

As you can see, typing actual process names can be tedious, especially if you're going to terminate a whole batch of them. So, to make them easier, the developers of Linux came up with the PID. Instead of typing the whole process name, you can just replace the actual process name with the PID. In our example, kacpi_hotplug's PID is 18. Therefore, the command syntax would be:

$ K 18

As you can see, typing the command with the PID is much faster and easier than typing the command with the actual process name. All processes in Linux have a unique PID. So, if one particular process is doing something that it is not supposed to be doing, it is extremely easy for the user to identify that process through the PID and terminate it.

For a more in-depth understanding of how the *top* command works, you can also press the letter *H* while in the task manager. Pressing *H* while within the Linux task manager will bring up a screen that enumerates all the different subcommands that you can use with the *top* command.

```
Help for Interactive Commands - procps version 3.2.8
Window 1:Def: Cumulative mode Off.  System: Delay 3.0 secs; Secure mode Off.

  2,B       Global: 'Z' change color mappings; 'B' disable/enable bold
  l,t,m     Toggle Summaries: 'l' load avg; 't' task/cpu stats; 'm' mem info
  1,I       Toggle SMP view: '1' single/separate states; 'I' Irix/Solaris mode

  f,o     . Fields/Columns: 'f' add or remove; 'o' change display order
  F or O  . Select sort field
  <,>     . Move sort field: '<' next col left; '>' next col right
  R,H     . Toggle: 'R' normal/reverse sort; 'H' show threads
  c,i,S   . Toggle: 'c' cmd name/line; 'i' idle tasks; 'S' cumulative time
  x,y     . Toggle highlights: 'x' sort field; 'y' running tasks
  z,b     . Toggle: 'z' color/mono; 'b' bold/reverse (only if 'x' or 'y')
  u       . Show specific user only
  n or #  . Set maximum tasks displayed

  k,r       Manipulate tasks: 'k' kill; 'r' renice
  d or s    Set update interval
  W         Write configuration file
  q         Quit
          ( commands shown with '.' require a visible task display window )
Press 'h' or '?' for help with Windows,
any other key to continue
```

Think of this screen as a help page for the *top* command. All the subcommands indicated in this help page only works within the *top* environment--while the Linux task manager is up and running.

Linux Services

A system restart is required every time you update system files, install programs, or change system settings in Microsoft Windows. Restarting ensures that the changes that you made get implemented successfully by the system. While restarting a running system ensures stability in the long run, it may become tedious and troublesome, especially if you have to wait for a particular running task to finish first before restarting.

With Linux, however, restarting the whole system is not required. Every time you go in and change system configuration files of a particular software in your Linux system, you may need to restart that individual software or that individual service only, not the whole system. This is one of the advantages Linux has over Windows.

Let us say you have the *Apache2* program installed into your Linux server, and you want to make some changes to the configuration files. The changes that you made in the configuration files do not get loaded until your restart the *Apache2* service. Even though the computer stays on all the time, you do have to restart the services every once in a while just to make sure they are up-to-date. What we are going to see now is how to start, stop and restart services in Linux.

Below are the three command syntaxes for starting, stop, or restarting a service in Linux:

$ sudo /etc/init.d/<name of the program or service > restart

$ sudo /etc/init.d/<name of the program or service > stop

$ sudo /etc/init.d/<name of the program or service> start

So, let us say you changed the configuration files in the *Apache2* program in your server and you need to restart it. All you need to do is type:

$ sudo /etc/init.d/Apache2 restart

This would restart the *Apache2* service, which would bring whatever configuration changes you have made. Now, let us say you are playing with the web server, you are making some changes, and you do not want anybody from the outside world coming in while you do the changes. So you want to stop the services entirely, which basically makes the web server go offline. All you do is:

$ sudo /etc/init.d/Apache2 stop

The above command stops the web service. However, it does not stop anything else. This means that while nobody from the outside world is able to reach the website that you are hosting, you are still able to make changes to the configuration files, edit options, modify settings, etc. Only the actual web server component is not functioning at this point.

Let us now go ahead and look at how this looks like when you actually execute it at the command prompt of Linux.

```
Welcome to the Ubuntu Server!
 * Documentation:  http://www.ubuntu.com/server/doc

  System information as of Fri Aug 20 11:42:30 EDT 2010

  System load:  0.14             Processes:          66
  Usage of /:   11.2% of 7.49GB  Users logged in:    0
  Memory usage: 14%              IP address for lo:  127.0.0.1
  Swap usage:   0%               IP address for eth0: 10.0.2.15

  Graph this data and manage this system at https://landscape.canonical.com/

  @server:~$
```

So right now we're at the command prompt or terminal of our Linux server operating system. In this example, let us assume that you have *Apache2* installed on your system, and that you want to stop that service. The first thing that you should do is type in the word *sudo*, put a space after the *sudo,* then type in */etc/init.d/Apache2*, put a space again after that, and then the word *stop*.

As soon as you hit ENTER after typing in the aforementioned command, you will get the below screen:

```
Welcome to the Ubuntu Server!
 * Documentation:  http://www.ubuntu.com/server/doc

  System information as of Fri Aug 20 11:42:30 EDT 2010

  System load:   0.14              Processes:          66
  Usage of /:    11.2% of 7.49GB   Users logged in:    0
  Memory usage:  14%               IP address for lo:  127.0.0.1
  Swap usage:    0%                IP address for eth0: 10.0.2.15

  Graph this data and manage this system at https://landscape.canonical.com/

  @server:~$ sudo /etc/init.d/apache2 stop
 * Stopping web server apache2
apache2: Could not reliably determine the server's fully qualified domain name,
using 127.0.1.1 for ServerName
 ... waiting                                                         [ OK ]
  @server:~$ _
```

As you can see in the screen above, Linux has successfully
stopped the service. At this point, the domain that this web
server is hosting is not accessible over the Internet. The
website is currently offline. To start the service, all you need to
do is type the same command that we typed when stopping the
service, with the exception of typing *start* instead of stop at the
end.

```
Welcome to the Ubuntu Server!
 * Documentation:  http://www.ubuntu.com/server/doc

  System information as of Fri Aug 20 11:42:30 EDT 2010

  System load:   0.14              Processes:          66
  Usage of /:    11.2% of 7.49GB   Users logged in:    0
  Memory usage:  14%               IP address for lo:  127.0.0.1
  Swap usage:    0%                IP address for eth0: 10.0.2.15

  Graph this data and manage this system at https://landscape.canonical.com/

  @server:~$ sudo /etc/init.d/apache2 stop
 * Stopping web server apache2
apache2: Could not reliably determine the server's fully qualified domain name,
using 127.0.1.1 for ServerName
 ... waiting                                                         [ OK ]
  @server:~$ sudo /etc/init.d/apache2 start
 * Starting web server apache2
apache2: Could not reliably determine the server's fully qualified domain name,
using 127.0.1.1 for ServerName
                                                                     [ OK ]
  @server:~$
```

When restarting a service--starting and stopping a service
automatically--all you need to do is enter the same command.
The only exception is instead of typing *start* or *stop* at the end,
you type *restart*. Again, what is incredibly nice about this is
the fact that you do not have to restart the entire server.

If you restart an entire server, no matter how fast the operating system is, it is going to take a couple of minutes before everything is online. If you only have to restart the service, everything will be back online in seconds.

Other Commands to Keep in Mind

There are various commands that can make the way you use Linux even easier and better. You can learn more about them below!

- **zip** Package and compress files.

- **yes** Print a string until interrupted

- **xz** Compress or decompress .xz and .lzma files

- **xdg-open** Open a file or URL in the user's preferred application.

- **xargs** Execute utility, passing constructed argument list(s)

- **write** Send a message to another user

- **whoami** Print the current user id and name (`id -un`)

- **who** Print all usernames currently logged in

- **while** Execute commands

- **which** Search the user's $path for a program file

- **whereis** Search the user's $path, man pages and source files for a program

- **wget** Retrieve web pages or files via HTTP, HTTPS or FTP

- **wc**   Print byte, word, and line counts
- **watch** Execute/display a program periodically
- **wait**   Wait for a process to complete •
- **vmstat** Report virtual memory statistics
- **vi**   Text Editor
- **vdir** Verbosely list directory contents (`ls -l -b')
- **Verbosely**list directory contents (`ls -l -b')
- **uuencode** Encode a binary file
- **uudecode** Decode a file created by uuencode
- **users**   List users currently logged in
- **usermod** Modify user account
- **userdel** Delete a user account
- **useradd** Create new user account
- **uptime**   Show uptime
- **until**   Execute commands (until error)
- **unshar**   Unpack shell archive scripts
- **unset**   Remove variable or function names
- **unrar**   Extract files from a rar archive
- **units**   Convert units from one scale to another
- **uniq**   Uniquify files
- **unexpand** Convert spaces to tabs

- **uname** Print system information

- **unalias** Remove an alias

- **umount** Unmount a device

- **umask** Users file creation mask

- **ulimit** Limit user resources •

- **type** Describe a command

- **tty** Print filename of terminal on stdin

- **tsort** Topological sort

- **true** Do nothing, successfully

- **trap** Run a command when a signal is set(bourne)

- **traceroute** Trace Route to Host

- **tr** Translate, squeeze, and/or delete characters

- **tput** Set terminal-dependent capabilities, color, position

- **touch** Change file timestamps

- **top** List processes running on the system

- **times** User and system times

- **timeout** Run a command with a time limit

- **time** Measure Program running time

- **test** Evaluate a conditional expression

- **tee**   Redirect output to multiple files

- **tar**   Store, list or extract files in an archive

- **tail**   Output the last part of file

- **sync** Synchronize data on disk with memory

- **suspend** Suspend execution of this shell

- **sum**   Print a checksum for a file

- **sudo**   Execute a command as another user

- **su**   Substitute user identity

- **strace**   Trace system calls and signals

- **stat**   Display file or file system status

- **ssh**   Secure Shell client

- **split**   Split a file into fixed-size pieces

- **source** Run commands from a file

- **sort**   Sort text files

- **slocate** Find files

- **sleep**   Delay for a specified time

- **shutdown** Shutdown or restart Linux

- Shell Options

- **shift**   Shift positional parameters

- **sftp**   Secure File Transfer Program

- **set**   Manipulate shell variables and functions

- **seq** Print numeric sequences
- **select** Accept keyboard input
- **sed** Stream Editor
- **sdiff** Merge two files interactively
- **screen** Multiplex terminal, run remote shells via ssh
- **scp** Secure copy or create remote file copy
- **rsync** Remote file copy
- **rmdir** Remove folder/s
- **rm** Remove files
- **rev** Reverse lines of a file
- **return** Exit a shell function
- **renice** Alter priority of running processes
- **rename** Rename files
- **remsync** Synchronize remote files via email
- **reboot** Reboot the system
- **readonly** Mark variables/functions as readonly
- **readarray** Read from stdin into an array variable
- **read** Read a line from standard input
- **rcp** Copy files between two machines
- **rar** Archive files with compression
- **ram** ram disk device

- **quotacheck** Scan a file system for disk usage

- **quota** Display disk usage and limits

- **pwd** Print Working Directory

- **pv** Monitor the progress of data through a pipe

- **pushd** Save and then change the current directory

- **ps** Process status

- **printf** Format and print data

- **printenv**

- Print environment variables

- **printcap** Printer capability database

- **pr**   Prepare files for printing

- **popd**   Restore the previous value of the current directory

- **pkill**   Kill processes by a full or partial name.

- **ping** Test a network connection

- **pathchk** Check file name portability

- **paste** Merge lines of files

- **passwd** Modify a user password

- **open** Open a file in its default application

- **op**   Operator access

- **nslookup** Query Internet name servers interactively

- **notify-send** Send desktop notifications

- **nohup**   Run a command immune to hangups

- **nl**   Number lines and write files

- **nice**   Set the priority of a command or job

- **netstat**   Networking information

- **nc**   Netcat, read and write data across networks

- **mv**   Move or rename files or directories

- **mtr**   Network diagnostics

- **mtools**   Manipulate MS-DOS files

- **mount**   Mount a file system

- **most**   Browse or page through a text file

- **more**   Display output one screen at a time

- **mmv**   Mass Move and rename file/s

- **mknod**   Make block or character special files

- **mkisofs**   Create an hybrid ISO9660/JOLIET/HFS filesystem

- **mkfifo**   Make FIFOs

- **mkdir**   Create new folder/s

- **make**   Recompile a group of programs

- **lsof**   List open files

- **ls**   List information about file/s

- **lprm**   Remove jobs from the print queue

- **lprintq**   List the print queue

102

- **lprintd** Abort a print job

- **lprint** Print a file

- **lpr** Off line print

- **lpc** Line printer control program

- **look** Display lines beginning with a given string

- **logout** Exit a login shell

- **logname** Print current login name

- **locate** Find files

- **local** Create variables

- **ln** Create a symbolic link to a file

- **link** Create a link to a file

- **let** Perform arithmetic on shell variables

- **less** Display output one screen at a time

- **killall** Kill processes by name

- **kill** Kill a process by specifying its PID

- **join** Join lines on a common field

- **jobs** List active jobs

- **ip** Routing, devices and tunnels

- **install** Copy files and set attributes

- **import** Capture an X server screen and save the image to file

- **ifup** Start a network interface up

- **ifdown** Stop a network interface

- **ifconfig** Configure a network interface

- **if** Conditionally perform a command

- *id* Print user and group id's

- **iconv** Convert the character set of a file

- **htop** Interactive process viewer

- **hostname** Print or set system name

- **history** Command History

- **help** Display help for a built-in command

- **head** Output the first part of file/s

- **hash** Remember the full pathname of a name argument

- **gzip** Compress or decompress named file/s

- **groups** Print group names a user is in

- **groupmod** Modify a group

- **groupdel** Delete a group

- **groupadd** Add a user security group

- **grep** Search file/s for lines that match a given pattern

- **getopts** Parse positional parameters

- **gawk** Find and Replace text within file/s

- **fuser** Identify/kill the process that is accessing a file

- **function** Define Function Macros

- **ftp**   File Transfer Protocol

- **fsck**   File system consistency check and repair

- **free**   Display memory usage

- **format**   Format disks or tapes

- **for**   Expand *words*, and execute *commands*

- **fold**   Wrap text to fit a specified width.

- **fmt**   Reformat paragraph text

- **find**   Search for files that meet a desired criteria

- **file**   Determine file type

- **fgrep**   Search file/s for lines that match a fixed string

- **fg**   Send job to foreground

- **fdisk**   Partition table manipulator for Linux

- **fdformat** Low-level format a floppy disk

- **false**   Do nothing, unsuccessfully

- **expr**   Evaluate expressions

- **export**   Set an environment variable

- **expect**   Automate arbitrary applications accessed over a terminal

- **expand**   Convert tabs to spaces

- **exit**   Exit the shell

- **exec**   Execute a command

- **eval**   Evaluate several commands/arguments

- **ethtool** Ethernet card settings

- **env**   Environment variables

- **enable** Enable and disable builtin shell commands

- **eject**   Eject removable media

- **egrep**   Search file(s) for lines that match an extended expression

- **echo**   Display message on screen

- **du**   Estimate file space usage

- **dmesg**   Print kernel & driver messages

- **dirs**   Display list of remembered directories

- **dirname** Convert a full pathname to just a path

- **dircolors** Colour setup for `ls'

- **dir**   Briefly list directory contents

- **dig**   DNS lookup

- **diff3**   Show differences among three files

- **diff**   Display the differences between two files

- **df**   Display free disk space

- **declare** Declare variables and give them attributes

- **ddrescue** Data recovery tool

- **dd**   Convert and copy a file, write disk headers, boot records

- **dc**   Desk Calculator

- **date**   Display or change the date & time

- **cut**   Divide a file into several parts

- **curl**   Transfer data from or to a server

- **csplit** Split a file into context-determined pieces

- **crontab** Schedule a command to run at a later time

- **cron**   Daemon to execute scheduled commands

- **cp**   Copy one or more files to another location

- **continue** Resume the next iteration of a loop

- **command** Run a command - ignoring shell functions

- **comm**   Compare two sorted files line by line

- **cmp**   Compare two files

- **clear**   Clear terminal screen

- **cksum**   Print CRC checksum and byte counts

- **chroot**   Run a command with a different root directory

- **chown**   Change file owner and group

- **chmod**   Change access permissions

- **chkconfig** System services

- **chgrp**   Change group ownership

- **cfdisk** Partition table manipulator for Linux

- **cd**   Change Directory

- **cat**   Concatenate and print the content of files

- **case**   Conditionally perform a command

- **cal**   Display a calendar

- **bzip2** Compress or decompress named file(s)

- **builtin** Run a shell builtin

- **break**   Exit from a loop

- **bind**   Set or display readline key and function bindings •

- **bg**   Send to background

- **bc**   Arbitrary precision calculator language

- **bash**   GNU Bourne-Again SHell

- **basename** Strip directory and suffix from filenames

- **awk**   Find and Replace text, database sort/validate/index

- **aspell** pell Checker

- **aptitude** Search for and install software packages (Debian/Ubuntu)

- **apt-get** Search for and install software packages (Debian/Ubuntu)

- **apropos** search help manual pages

- **alias**   Create an alias

Loops and Statements

There are three types of loops and they are:

- **For Loop.** This is when statements are executed a multiple number of times and codes are abbreviated.

- **While Loop.** This is when statements or groups of statements are repeated when conditions are said to be true.

- **Nested Loop.** This means you're using loops inside or above the first few loops.

- You can also make use of Loop Control Statements, such as:

- **Continue Statement.** This makes the loop skip the rest of its body and resets it back to its original form.

- **Break Statement.** This transfers statement execution before terminating the loop, and immediately brings back the other loop. For example:

- **Pass Statement.** When you do not want to execute codes or commands for syntax, that's what you call a pass statement.

- **==.** Condition equates to true if the operands are equal. ((a==b) is not true)

- **<>.** If values are not equal, condition becomes true. ((a<>b) is true)

- **!=.** Condition becomes true if values of two operands are not equal.

- **<=.** Condition becomes true if left operand value is less than the right operand. (a <=b) is true)

- **>=.** Condition becomes true if value of left operand is greater than right operand. (a>=b) is not true)

- **<.** If left operand value is less than right operand, condition is true. (a < b) is true)

- **>.** If value of left operand is greater than right, condition is true. ((a>b is not true)

Linux Lexicon

In Linux, Dictionaries are considered as hash tables or associative arrays. They are filled up with numbers and strings. They are enclosed by curly braces {{}} and values are assigned by square braces [].

Numbers in Linux

Of course, you can expect that numbers are used to store numerical values. Assign your preferred numbers to the variables. For example:

var1 = 1

var2 = 10

You can also make use of the following numerical types:

- Int (signed integers)

- Complex (complex numbers)

- Float (floating real point values)

- Long (long integers; could be hexadecimal and octal)

Classes in Linux

Classes determine the scope of the program, which are:

- Local names, or innermost scope;

- Built-in names and words last searched, or outermost scope;

- Current global module names or next to last scope, and;

- Enclosing Function scope.

Lists in Linux

Linux also allows you to create lists that could be enclosed in brackets {[]}. They are like the same lists used in C Language, but are definitely easier to make. Again, make use of slice operators ([] or [:]), and start with indexes of 0. You can concentrate the strings by using the plus sign (+) and repeat by using the asterisk (*).

Linux Loops

There are three types of loops and they are:

- **For Loop.** This is when statements are executed a multiple number of times and codes are abbreviated.

- **While Loop.** This is when statements or groups of statements are repeated when conditions are said to be true.

- **Nested Loop.** This means you're using loops inside or above the first few loops.

- You can also make use of Loop Control Statements, such as:

- **Continue Statement.** This makes the loop skip the rest of its body and resets it back to its original form.

- **Break Statement.** This transfers statement execution before terminating the loop, and immediately brings back the other loop. For example:

- **Pass Statement.** When you do not want to execute codes or commands for syntax, that's what you call a pass statement.

Right Values

The equal sign (=) is important here because. You do not need to make explicit declarations here but you have to make sure that you place the variable before the equal sign, and on the right, put what you want to happen to the variable.

A Tuple is like list data but is composed of a lot of values that are separated by commas, and are enclosed in parentheses () as opposed to brackets. Tuples also cannot be updated.

Conversions of Diff.erent Data Types

- **Unichr (x).** And finally, with this command, you'll get a Unicode character.

- **Tuple (t).** Converts x to tuple.

- **Str (x).** converts x to string representation.

- **Set (s).** Converts x to set.

- **Repr (x).** Converts x to repression string.

- **Ord (x).** This gives a single character its integer value.

- **Oct (x).** Converts x to octal string.

- **Long (x [,base]).** Converts x to long integers.

- **List (L).** Converts x to list.

- **Int (x [,base]).** If x is a string, it becomes the base; also converts x to an integer.

- **Hex (x).** Converts x to hexadecimal string.

- **Frozen set (s).** Converts x to frozen set.

- **Float (x).** Converts integers into floating numbers.

- **Eval (str).** This evaluates a string and gives you an object in return.

- **Dict (d).** This gives you a dictionary.

- **Complex (real [,imag]).** This gives you a complex number.

Built-in Strings

In order to program those, you have to make use of special characters and codes. These are:

Built-in String Method

- **Zfill (width).** Left-pads original string with zeros.

- **Upper ().** Turns lowercase letters into uppercase.

- **Translate (table, deletechars**="") Turns string into translation table.

- **Title ().** Turns string into titlecard version, which means uppercase becomes lowercase and vice-versa.

- **Swapcase ().** All letters in the string will be inverted.

- **Strip ([chars]).** Performs rstrip() and Istrip() on each string.

- **Startswith (str, beg=0, end=len (string)).** Checks whether string is string itself or subset of string.

- **Splitlines (num=string.count('\n')).** Returns each of the line with new strings.

- **Split (str="", num=string.count (str)).** Splits the strings into delimeters.

- **Rjust (width, [,fillchar]).** This gives you space-padded strings.

- **Rindex (str, beg=0, end=len(string)).** This is just like index but with backward string.

- **Replace (old, new [max]).** This replaces current string with max occurrences.

- **Max (str).** This returns max character alphabetical string.

- **Join (seq).** This merges representations of the strings.

- **Isdecimal().** If Unicode string contains decimal characters, value returns as true; false otherwise.

- **Find (str, beg=0, end=len(string)).** This checks whether str is on string or on subsequent string.

- **Expandtabs (tabsize = 8).** Strings and tabs are then placed in multiple spaces.

- **Encode (suffix, beg=0, end=len(string)).** This runs an encoded version of each string.

- **Decode (encoding UTF-8, errors=strict).** The codec registered for encoding will be used for this method, and you'd get a default string.

- **Count (str, beg=0, end=len(string)).** This counts the number of times a string appears and begins indexing.

- **Center (width, fillchar).** Along with the original string, this'll give you a space-padded string consuming the total width of the columns.

- **Capitalize().** This basically capitalizes the first letter of the string.

Symbols for Formatting

- **m.n.** m is the minimum total width and n is the number of digits to display after the decimal point (if appl.)

- pad from left with zeros (instead of spaces)

- **<sp>.** leave a blank space before a positive number

- **+.** display the sign

- ***.** argument specifies width or precision

- **(var).** mapping variable (dictionary arguments)

- **%.** '%%' leaves you with a single literal '%'

- **#.** add the octal leading zero ('o') or hexadecimal leading 'ox' or 'oX', depending on whether 'x' or 'X' were used.

- **-.** left justification

- %X   hexadecimal integer (UPPERcase letters)

- %x   hexadecimal integer (lowercase letters)

- %u   unsigned decimal integer

- %s   string conversion via str() prior to formatting

- %o   octal integer

- %i   signed decimal integer

- %g   the shorter of %f and %e

- %G   the shorter of %f and %E

- %f   floating point real number

- %E   exponential notation (with UPPERcase 'E')

- %e   exponential notation (with lowercase 'e')

- %d   signed decimal integer

- %c   character

Chapter 10: File Editing

Editing files is one of the most important things you need to learn in order to be proficient in Linux. In this chapter, we're going to learn how to edit files in Linux using the Vim text editor. As what we've mentioned in the earlier chapters, one of the main advantages of Linux is its customizability--to be able to make the operating system work other than what was originally intended.

Customization in Linux often involves opening a small configuration text file and editing the values within. In order to open a configuration file successfully, one must use a text editor. EVE, Emacs, LSE, and Textadept are just some of the many text editors that are available for Linux out there. However, the text editor most people recommend using--due to its versatility and ease of use--is *Vim*.

One of the big things that you have to understand since most of you are coming from the Windows operating system is that in Linux, there are no file associations. What we mean by this is in Windows, you always have the file extension--association--after the filename. For example, if you have a Microsoft Word document named *Notes*, you will notice that the file extension that it will have is either *.doc* or *.docx*. Therefore, its complete filename would be either *Notes.doc,* or *Notes.docx.*

The file extension is what tells the Windows operating system what program to use to open that file. In Linux, there are no file associations. This is one of the main reasons why most people are afraid of using Linux; no file associations at all. Basically, all you have is just a filename. That is it.

Now you may be asking: how do you know if it is a text file or any other file type? Well, that is the weird thing in Linux. They expect you, as the system administrator, to know what that file is.

So if you are going to modify text files, understand that they are not going to have *.txt* file extensions. It will just be the filename. You must understand what file it is you need to modify first before you use a file editor software to edit that file.

All the configuration files in Linux have to be edited using a file editor. If you do not understand how to edit documents or texts in Linux, you are not going to get anywhere.

Starting the Vim Text Editor

Before we start editing files using *Vim*, we must first learn how to start and open files with it. Starting *Vim,* and opening files with it, is pretty straightforward. All you have to do is type the syntax below:

> $ sudo vim <name of the file you want to create or open>

So first, we must type in the *sudo*, and then a space, followed by the word *vim,* and then another space, and then followed by the name of the file that you want to open or create.

In Linux, capitalization is important. So, when you're typing the word *vim,* make sure that it is all in lowercase. If you type *vim* in other than all lowercase, Linux won't be able to understand the command since as far as Linux is concern, the executable file of the Vim text editor is not typed with an uppercase letter.

Capitalization also applies to files that you want to open or access in Linux. If the filename of the file that you want to open has an uppercase letter, then type it as such. Type the filenames of files accordingly to avoid any errors in Linux.

Now, let us say that you want to open and edit a file named *php.ini*. To open the *php.ini* file, type the syntax below:

$ sudo vim php.ini

Vim's capability is not only limited to opening and editing existing files in Linux. It can also create new files. The syntax for creating new files using Vim is pretty much the same as when you're opening an existing file.

$ sudo vim <name of the new file that you want to create>

The only difference is that, if you're creating a new file, make sure that the filename you're going to use doesn't exist in the first place. If you do make use of an existing filename, you'll be opening that filename rather than creating a new one.

Note that the use of the *sudo* prefix to execute the command to start Vim is not required. The problem with running *Vim* without *sudo,* at least in the Ubuntu distribution, is sometimes it will work right, and sometimes it will not. It is a case-to-case basis where some of the configuration files will open and can be edited without using sudo, while others will not edit properly.

Also, you'll most likely to encounter the problem where if you were to open a configuration file with simply *vim* and the filename, you will not be able to save the file once you are finished editing it. Why? Because you did not open that file as an administrator. This is why it is always considered good practice to use *sudo* whenever you are doing critical tasks in Linux.

File Ownership

File ownership is another important thing that we need to take note of when using *Vim* to edit configuration files. What do we basically mean by file ownership? Well, keep in mind that most of the software that you install on your Linux system came from their respective developers. In other words, they came from an external source. When you install them onto your Linux system, the ownership of all the files of that software technically still falls on the developer.

Now, here is the problem: In Linux, you cannot edit any file unless you are the owner of that file. For example, when you install *Apache2, mySQL,* or *PHP* on your Linux web server, all the files associated with that software is owned by the administrator of the source file. If you try to go in and edit some of those files, it is very likely that you will not be able to edit them because you are not the owner.

So, if you are going to edit configuration files in Linux, the first thing that you ought to do is change the ownership of that file to you. To do that, you simply type in this command:

$ sudo chown <username> <filename>

The *username* in the above command pertains to the name of the user that you want to change the permission to. *Filename,* on the other hand, pertains to the name of the file that you want to change the ownership to.

Let us say your username is *user1* and you want to change the ownership of the file named *filenotes*. All you need to do is type the command syntax below:

$ sudo chown user1 filenotes

Once you do this, you will now become the owner of the file and thus will have the ability or permission to edit it.

File Editing and Navigation

Now that we have finished discussing how to open and create files using Vim, the next thing we need to learn is how to edit or modify configuration files with it. When you open a file for editing using Vim, you'll notice that even though you start typing the changes that you want to make, nothing will happen. This is one of the security measures incorporated in Vim.

This prevents accidental changes to be implemented in a configuration file. So, to make and implement changes in a file, you must first go into *Insert* mode. To go into *Insert* mode in Vim, you have to press the letter *A*. After pressing letter *A*, any changes that you make will be written on the file.

Once you're done making changes in the file, the next thing that you have to do is get out of *Insert* mode. To do this, you must press the *Esc* key on your keyboard. It is that simple.

There will be times when you also have to edit main configuration files in Linux. These main configuration files will almost always contain more than a hundred lines of code; they are really long documents. Now, what if you only need to edit a single word or value in that main configuration file? Surely you don't want to go through every single line of code just to look for that one value that you need to change; it will be extremely tedious.

Luckily, Vim offers users a search function, so that they do not need to go through every single line of code just to find that single value or word that they want to edit.

In order to call up Vim's search function, you must first make sure that you're out of *Insert* mode. Once you're out of *Insert* mode, type the command syntax below:

> :/ <name of value or word that you want to change>

That is colon, followed by a forward slash, and then a space, and then word or value that you are looking for within the file that you are trying to modify. Again, remember that capitalization is crucial. Make sure that the capitalization of the entry that you're looking for is correct, or else Linux will not able to find it. And if it does find it, it will be the incorrect one.

So, what this search command does in Vim is search for the keyword or value in the whole document, starting from where your cursor is situated within the file. If your blinking cursor is situated at the beginning of the file, then it will start searching from there.

For example, let's say you're looking for the word *else* within the configuration file. To look for the word *else*, your search command syntax should be like this:

:/ else

Now, here's the problem with the search command in *Vim*: Sometimes, Vim will not display any result if there is a space or another character before or after the string that you're searching for. If, let's say, you're looking for words within the file that has the string *"and"* within them--words like *command, stranded,* etc.--then there's a chance that the normal search command syntax in Vim will not yield any result.

To circumvent this problem, Vim developers allowed the use of wildcard characters when executing search commands in Vim. Going back to our previously mentioned example, if you're looking for every word that has the string *"and"* within them, your search command syntax should be like this:

> :/ *and*

The above search command syntax basically tells Vim that you're looking for the string *"and"* within the document regardless of its prefix or suffix. We mentioned previously that the search command looks for the keyword or value that you're looking for starting from the position of the cursor. Now, what if the search didn't find anything and your cursor is now positioned at the end of the file?

To execute a search upwards from where your cursor is currently positioned, you must type the search command syntax below:

:/? <name of string or value that you're looking for>

That is colon, followed by a forward slash, followed by a question mark, a space, and then the string or value that you are looking for. This is what will make the search go upwards from where your cursor is at.

Now, what if there are multiple instances of the string or value that you are looking for in a *vim* file? Well, when you do a search, *Vim* will automatically halt on the first instance of the string or value that you are looking for. To move to the next instance, you just need to hit the letter "*n*" on the keyboard. This is the equivalent of "Find Next" in the Windows operating system.

As you can see, navigating in *Vim* is really easy. The above commands are all it takes to open, navigate, search, and edit files in *Vim*.

Saving Your Changes and Exiting Vim

The next thing we need to talk about is how to open, exit, and save files within *Vim*. So far, we have discussed opening *Vim* files from the command prompt. So now, let us discuss how to open up other *Vim* files while inside *Vim* itself.

If you need to open a file and you are already in *Vim*--so you need to switch to another file--all you need to do is type the command below:

    :e <filename>

That is a colon, followed by a lowercase letter *e*, a space, and then the file name. Again, make sure you are out of *Insert* mode when you do this. If you are in *Insert* mode and you type in this command, what will happen is *Vim* will just type in the command within the file itself. It will not be interpreted as a command to open up a different file.

That is all you have to do to open up another *Vim* file from within *Vim*. Now, let us say you open up a file and you look around in them. But then, you decide that you do not want to change anything and you need to get out of that file. What you do in this instance is type in the command below:

:q

That is a colon, and then followed by the lowercase letter *q*. This command will exit you out of *Vim*. Of course, you have to press ENTER after typing in each command in order to execute them.

There will be times when you also have to force quit out of *Vim*. There may be times when *Vim* has become unresponsive or it does not want to accept the normal quit command. In cases like these, you want to force *Vim* to exit. To do that you have to put an exclamation mark after the lowercase letter *q*.

:q!

Whether *Vim* got stuck or has become unresponsive to other commands, putting an exclamation mark after the lowercase letter *q* will definitely get you out of the *Vim* application. Only use this command if nothing else works. Keep in mind that if you are quitting *Vim* normally using the *:q* or *:q!* command, no changes will be saved in the file that you are trying to edit. Not unless, you saved the changes first before trying to execute the quit command.

Now, let us say *Vim* locked up for some reason and you have already entered numerous changes in the file. Of course, in order for you not to go through all the changes again, you want to save the file before quitting. In this instance, what you do is type in the command below:

:wq

That is a colon, followed by the lowercase letter *w*, and then followed by the lowercase letter *q*. The lowercase letter *w* stands for "write", while the lowercase letter *q* stands for quit. So this will save whatever changes you made to the file first before quitting *Vim*.

The next thing is, let us say you made some changes to the file but you do not want it to be saved to the original file. So you are basically trying to do a "save as" command here. To do that, just type in the command below:

:w <new filename>

That is colon, followed by a lowercase letter *w*, a space, and then the name of the new file that you want to create and save into. This command will save the file that you edited to a new file. This is particularly useful when you do not want to overwrite the original file and you want to preserve it for some reason.

Chapter 11: Linux Directory Navigation

Now we need to talk about basic folder/directory navigation in the Linux operating system. Managing Linux files and directories would help you keep things in check. As with any kind of Operating system, it is important to make sure that you know what's happening to your system so that it would not disintegrate. More so, it is a way of being mindful of the things you have in your system. Learn more about them in this chapter!

This is slightly different than Microsoft Windows. But the funny thing is, it looks close enough to Windows that when things do not work right, people have a nasty tendency of wanting to pick up their computer and throw it out the window. Consider the directory hierarchy illustration below.

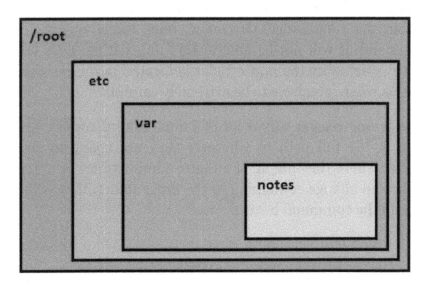

In Linux, you have the *cd* command just like in Windows. The *cd* command stands for change directory. If you want to go to a different directory or folder, you type in *cd*. If you are in a folder, let us say you are in the *var* folder in our illustration, and you want to go to a folder within the *var* folder, which in this case is the *notes* folder, all you need to do is type in the command below:

$ cd notes

So, that is *cd,* a space, and then the name of the folder that you want to go to. That will drop you in the folder that you are trying to go into. Now, the problem is, people in the Windows world are used to following the *cd* command with a forward slash symbol. If we were to apply this in our previous command, it will look like the one below:

$ cd /notes

What Linux does in this case is, it interprets the forward slash symbol as the *root* folder. Linux will think that you want to change to the *root* folder, and then look for the *notes* folder within the *root* folder. Of course, once Linux executes this command, it will not be able to find an existing *notes* folder since in actuality the *notes* folder is located in the *var* folder. That is where you have to be extremely careful.

This is one reason why a lot of Linux administrators always type in the full path to wherever they are trying to go, no matter where they are at. If a Linux administrator is trying to go in and change something in the *notes* folder, they will just type in the command below:

$ cd /etc/var/notes

Linux is finicky about this whole change directory syntax. As we have mentioned before as well, capitalization matters in Linux. If you are trying to reach a folder whose name is written

128

in all lowercase, and you type the folder in all capital letters, Linux will not be able to find it; it will say that the directory cannot be found.

Believe us when we say that all of this is important to understand. It can be extremely frustrating if you do not grasp it.

```
Welcome to the Ubuntu Server!
 * Documentation:  http://www.ubuntu.com/server/doc

  System information as of Fri Aug 20 11:57:13 EDT 2010

  System load:  0.0          Processes:          66
  Usage of /:   11.2% of 7.49GB  Users logged in:    0
  Memory usage: 14%           IP address for lo:   127.0.0.1
  Swap usage:   0%            IP address for eth0: 10.0.2.15

  Graph this data and manage this system at https://landscape.canonical.com/

  @server:~$ cd /_
```

So, the first thing you want to do when navigating files and folders in Linux is make sure that you are in the root directory. To do this, you must type the command below:

$ cd /

That is *cd,* a space, and then a forward slash. This will automatically bring you to the *root* directory if you are not yet there. Now the next logical thing to do would be to see what folders are within the *root* folder itself. To do this, you must type the command below:

$ ls

The *ls,* or list command will list all the files and folders within a particular directory--*root,* in this case.

129

```
Welcome to the Ubuntu Server!
 * Documentation:  http://www.ubuntu.com/server/doc

  System information as of Fri Aug 20 11:57:13 EDT 2010

  System load:  0.0          Processes:           66
  Usage of /:   11.2% of 7.49GB  Users logged in:     0
  Memory usage: 14%          IP address for lo:   127.0.0.1
  Swap usage:   0%           IP address for eth0: 10.0.2.15

  Graph this data and manage this system at https://landscape.canonical.com/

  @server:~$ cd /
  @server:/$ ls
bin     dev     initrd.img  lost+found  opt    sbin    sys   var
boot    etc     lib         media       proc   selinux tmp   vmlinuz
cdrom   home    lib64       mnt         root   srv     usr
  @server:/$ _
```

As you can see after typing in the *ls* command, Linux will now
show you all the folders that are within in the *root* directory.
You can see lots of folders here like the *bin, dev, opt, sbin, sys,
var, boot, etc lib,* and so forth.

Now, let us say we want to go inside the *etc* folder. All you
need to do is type in the command below:

$ cd etc

The command above will automatically drop you inside the *etc*
folder. If you look beside the blinking cursor of the command
prompt, it will say */etc$*. That is the main indication that you
are indeed inside the actual folder that you want to go into. If
you do the *ls* command again, it will show you all the files
within the *etc* folder.

```
apparmor              insserv.conf          python
apparmor.d            insserv.conf.d        python2.6
apport                iproute2              rc0.d
apt                   iscsi                 rc1.d
at.deny               issue                 rc2.d
at.deny               issue                 rc2.d
bash.bashrc           issue.net             rc3.d
bash_completion       kbd                   rc4.d
bash_completion.d     kernel-img.conf       rc5.d
bindresvport.blacklist landscape           rc6.d
blkid.conf            ldap                  rc.local
blkid.tab             ld.so.cache           rcS.d
byobu                 ld.so.conf            resolv.conf
ca-certificates       ld.so.conf.d          rmt
ca-certificates.conf  legal                 rpc
calendar              locale.alias          rsyslog.conf
chatscripts           localtime             rsyslog.d
console-setup         logcheck              screenrc
cron.d                login.defs            securetty
cron.daily            logrotate.conf        security
cron.hourly           logrotate.d           services
cron.monthly          lsb-base              sgml
crontab               lsb-base-logging.sh   shadow
cron.weekly           lsb-release           shadow-
dbus-1               ltrace.conf           shells
debconf.conf          magic                 skel
debian_version        magic.mime            ssh
default               mailcap               ssl
deluser.conf          mailcap.order         sudoers
depmod.d              manpath.config        sudoers.d
```

In order to go back to the *root* folder, all you need to do is type:

    $ cd /

This will automatically return you to the *root* directory no matter how deep you are within the folders.

Now let us say you want to go back to the *etc* folder. But this time, instead of typing *etc* in all lowercase, you typed it in all uppercase.

```
@server:/etc$ cd /
@server:/$ ls
bin    dev    initrd.img  lost+found  opt   sbin     sys   var
boot   etc    lib         media       proc  selinux  tmp   vmlinuz
cdrom  home   lib64       mnt         root  srv      usr
@server:/$ cd ETC
-bash: cd: ETC: No such file or directory
```

As you can see, Linux will not be able to find the directory with an uppercase *ETC*. Why? Because Linux cares about capitalization. Uppercase letters are different from lower case letters in the Linux world. Basically, that is all there is to it in Linux basic navigation.

Directories of Addresses

As the name suggests, this is a telecommunications protocol that makes it easy for communication apps and websites to work. It is used to map network addresses, making messaging—and even video calls—possible, and has also been used for important technologies, such as *Xerox PARC Universal Packet, DEC Net, ChaosNet,* and *IPv4,* amongst others. For this, you could keep in mind the following:

1. 0 – Hardware Type (HTYPE)

2. 2 – Protocol Type (PTYPE)

3. 4 – Hardware Address (HLEN) | Protocol Address (PLEN)

4. 6 – Operation (OPER)

5. 8 – Sender Hardware Address (SHA)

6. 10 - Next 2 succeeding bytes

7. 12 – Last 2 succeeding bytes

8. 14 – Sender Address Protocol (SAP)

9. 16 – last 2 succeeding bytes

10. 18 – Target Hardware Address (THA)

11. 20 – next 2 succeeding bytes

12. 22 – last 2 succeeding bytes

13. 24 – Target Protocol Address (TPA)

14. 26 – last 2 succeeding bytes

Transport Directories

The Transport Directories contains the channels of data that are involved in Linux, which also establishes process-to-process connectivity and end-to-end message transfers that provide the right information and logistics for any specific purpose in the network. This could either be implemented, connectionless, or object-oriented.

The port is then established with the help of the transport layer where logical constructs are around. It basically means that:

1. Data should be correct—and could only have minimal error;

2. Data should arrive in order;

3. Data should include traffic congestion control;

4. Packets that are discarded or lost have to be resent, and;

5. Duplicate data has to be discarded.

When that happens, you could expect even the newest version of the Stream Control Protocol to work properly in your network. You don't have to rely on connectionless datagrams, though, because as the name suggests, they don't offer the right connections—and are quite unreliable.

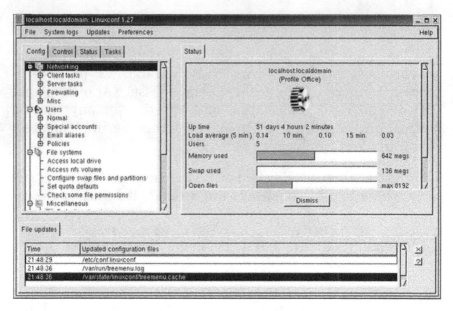

Application Directories

The Application Directories encapsulates the protocols used by services that provide exchanging applications. This also includes host configuration protocols, routing services and network support services. Examples include File Transfer Protocol (FTP), Hypertext Transfer Protocol (HTTP), and Dynamic Host Configuration Protocol (DHCP). This way, you would be able to lower data transfer based on the protocols you are using.

Application layer also treats the Transport Directories as a stable network with black boxes that allow communication to happen all throughout the application, while making sure that key qualities of each part of the application still work as strong as they can. Whatever happens to the Application Directories does not concern the Transport and Internet layers because traffic does not usually examine the said layer. However, sometimes, it is essential for the NAT, or Network Address

Translator, to consider the payload of the application—and make sure that things are running smoothly.

Chapter 12: Advanced Linux Directory Navigation

In the previous chapter, we already discussed how to change directories in Linux. In this chapter, we'll go into more advance directory commands. Now, we'll talk about how to create and delete directories, search for specific folders in Linux, and lastly, how to copy files.

Finding Files and Changing Directories

Back in chapter 10, we talked about how to edit configuration files using *Vim,* which is pretty essential in Linux. Now, as you sit there and look at the file system, you probably have no idea where those configuration files are in the first place. If you wanted to edit the *php.ini* file for example, the question that you may be asking since you are a beginner in Linux is: Where is the *php.ini* file located?

So, to find any particular file that you want to edit, you must first learn how to get to the folder or directory where that particular file is located. Again, to change directories, all you need to do is make use of the *cd* command just like in Windows. The syntax to change directory is:

    $ cd <name of folder>

Now, there is more to this command than meets the eye. Remember, Linux is exceptionally literal when it comes to the interpretation of command syntaxes. Again, let us make use of the diagram below:

136

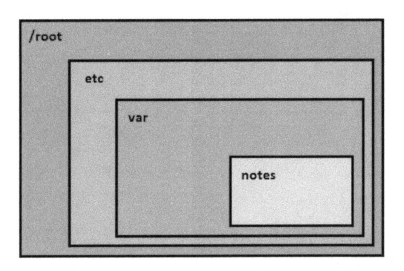

If for example you are in the *var* directory/folder and you want to go to the *abc* folder, all you need to do is type:

$ cd abc

Now, if for example you are in the *var* folder and you want to go to the *etc* folder, just typing in *$ cd etc* from within *var* will not work. Because then Linux will think that you want to go to the *etc* folder that is within the *var* folder, which does not exist.

What you must do is type the command below:

$ cd /etc

Take note of the forward slash before the name of the directory that you want to go to. This forward slash will tell Linux to first go to the *root* directory and then find the *etc* folder or directory. Now, Linux will now be able to successfully bring you to the *etc* folder since it is able to locate it in the *root* directory.

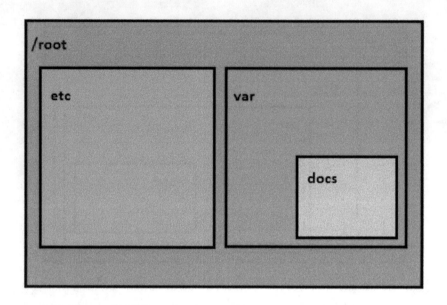

Consider the example illustration above. Let's say, for example, you're currently in the *root* directory and you want to go to the *docs* directory. If you type the syntax below:

    $ cd docs

Linux will return a *"file or directory does not exist"* error. Why would it return an error? Well, because there is no *docs* directory from where you're searching from. Remember, you're still inside the *root* directory. If you just type:

    $ cd docs

It's just basically telling Linux to look for the *docs* directory from your current location. It will return an error because *etc* and *var* are the only directories that exist within the *root* directory. As per our example illustration, the *docs* directory is located within the *var* directory, which is in turn within the *root* directory.

So, to successfully change to the *docs* directory from *root,* the command syntax should be like this:

$ cd /var/docs

Now you might be asking, won't the second forward slash in the above command bring you back to *root*? No, it will not. Linux only interprets the first instance of the forward slash as the *root* directory. The second forward slash will be interpreted as an instruction to look for the directory that succeeds it, from the directory that precedes it.

Now, let us say that you're in the *docs* directory and you want to go to the *etc* directory. If you just type:

$ cd etc

This command will obviously not work from within the *docs* directory. Why? Because again, as far as Linux is concerned, there is no *etc* directory inside the *docs* directory that you're currently in. So, to be able to successfully go to the *etc* directory from the *docs* directory, you must type the command syntax below:

$ cd /etc

As what we've mentioned before, only the first instance of the forward slash symbol will be recognized by Linux as a command to go to the *root* directory first. Once it is inside the *root* directory, it will now bring you inside the *etc* directory since it exists within the *root* directory.

Displaying/Listing Files Within a Directory

Since you're now able to navigate to any particular directory within Linux, the next thing you should do is find out what files are within that particular directory. Displaying the files that are within a particular directory is called *Listing*. To list the files that are inside a particular directory in Linux, you simply use the *ls* command.

$ ls

And then, depending on what you want to do, you can apply one of two arguments. If you do:

$ ls -l

What will happen is that all the files and folders will get listed. In addition to that, it will also show you the permissions for those files and folders, the date they were modified, the group ownership of the files and folders, and the individual owner.

```
@server:~$ ls -l
total 92
drwxr-xr-x   2 root root  4096 2010-08-17 12:39 bin
drwxr-xr-x   3 root root  4096 2010-08-17 12:41 boot
drwxr-xr-x   2 root root  4096 2010-08-17 12:31 cdrom
drwxr-xr-x  16 root root  3480 2010-09-13 15:35 dev
drwxr-xr-x  82 root root  4096 2010-09-14 01:12 etc
drwxr-xr-x   3 root root  4096 2010-08-17 12:42 home
lruxrwxrwx   1 root root    32 2010-08-17 12:32 initrd.img -> boot/initrd.img-2.6
.32-21-server
drwxr-xr-x  13 root root 12288 2010-08-24 11:22 lib
lruxrwxrwx   1 root root     4 2010-08-17 12:29 lib64 -> /lib
drwx------   2 root root 16384 2010-08-17 12:29 lost+found
drwxr-xr-x   2 root root  4096 2010-08-17 12:29 media
drwxr-xr-x   2 root root  4096 2010-04-23 06:23 mnt
drwxr-xr-x   2 root root  4096 2010-08-17 12:29 opt
dr-xr-xr-x  79 root root     0 2010-09-13 15:35 proc
drwx------   4 root root  4096 2010-08-17 12:35 root
drwxr-xr-x   2 root root  4096 2010-08-18 11:24 sbin
drwxr-xr-x   2 root root  4096 2009-12-05 17:25 selinux
drwxr-xr-x   2 root root  4096 2010-08-17 12:29 srv
drwxr-xr-x  13 root root     0 2010-09-13 15:35 sys
drwxr-xr-x   2 root root  4096 2010-08-23 14:08 test
drwxrwxrwt   2 root root  4096 2010-09-13 15:35 tmp
drwxr-xr-x  10 root root  4096 2010-08-17 12:29 usr
drwxr-xr-x  15 root root  4096 2010-08-18 11:37 var
lruxrwxrwx   1 root root    29 2010-08-17 12:32 vmlinuz -> boot/vmlinuz-2.6.32-21
```

A lot of times that can turn into a really big file. So, what you can also do is type:

$ ls -m

This time, instead of Linux giving you a really long list, it just types everything into a nice block so you can see every bit of information about the files and folders. That is all you need to do to list files and folders in Linux.

Now, let us say you want to edit a critical configuration file, but you have absolutely no idea where that file is. Thankfully, Linux does have a search option. In order to search for files and folders, all you do is type:

$ sudo find -iname <file/folder name>

That is *sudo,* a space, followed by the word *find,* another space, the argument *-iname*, another space, and then finally the name of the file or folder that you are looking for. Now you might be asking, what does that *-iname* argument do? Well, what it does is it makes the search case insensitive.

Remember, just like what we have been mentioning since chapter 1, capitalization matters in Linux. Since you are new to Linux, you may not know what files have uppercase letters and what files have lowercase letters. If you put in the *-iname* argument in your search parameter, it will locate the file or folder that you are looking for regardless of their capitalization.

If you are looking for a folder named *home* for example, and you use the search command with the *-iname* argument, it will come back with all the folder that has *home* as the folder name. Whether that folder is name as *Home, homE, hOme, HOme, hoMe,* or *HOME,* it will come up in the search result.

Whereas if you mess up the capitalization of the name of the file or folder that you are looking for, and you did not use the -*iname* argument, the search may come back with no results because no file or folder match the capitalization.

Also, do not forget about the *sudo* command when executing *find* commands in Linux. If you do not put in *sudo* at the beginning, the *find* command will fail in the most obnoxious way in that it will not tell you that it failed. It will simply not give you any results. So you will think that the file does not exist on the computer, when in actuality it does exist but you just did not use *sudo*.

With whatever file or folder that you are looking for, you can also use wildcard characters together with their name when doing a search. In chapter 6, we briefly talked about making use of the asterisk wildcard when searching for strings in *Vim*. When finding files and folders within the Linux file system, you can also make use of the asterisk wildcard.

If you put an asterisk before a file or folder name, that means that you are looking for "*anything before*" that particular file or folder name. Let us say you are trying to locate a configuration file in Linux. In Linux, all configuration files have .*conf* suffix. If you are looking for a configuration file but you forgot what the exact name is, you may want to pull up all the files that have .*conf* as their suffix. In this case, what you do is type the command below:

    $ sudo find -iname *.conf

What this command will do is to look for a file or folder name that begins with anything and ends with .*conf*. Now, what if you know the filename of the file that you are looking for, but you do not know the suffix. In this case, you need to type the command below:

$ sudo find -iname php*

What this command will do is look for a file or folder name that begins with *php* and ends with anything.

Creating, Renaming, Copying, Deleting, and Moving Files and Folders

Now that you know how to look for files within directories, we'll talk about how to create, rename, copy, delete, and move files and folders within Linux. First, let's discuss how to create a directory or folder. Creating a directory/folder is pretty easy. All you need to do is type the command syntax below:

$ sudo mkdir <name of folder/directory>

That is *sudo,* followed by a space, and then the *mkdir* parameter, another space, and then the name of the folder or directory that you want to make. As you may have already guessed, *mkdir* stands for "make directory."

Keep in mind that if you do not put the full path of the directory, this command will simply create that directory or folder inside the directory that you are currently in.

Now, let's say you're inside the *var* directory/folder and you want to make a directory named *notes* inside the *etc* folder. If you type the syntax below:

$ sudo mkdir notes

This command will just make a *notes* directory inside the *var* folder.

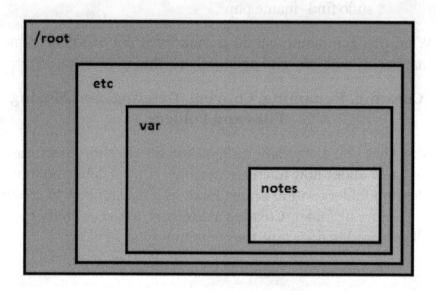

In order to create the *notes* directory inside the *etc* directory, you must type the path that points to the exact location where you want to create it, just like the command syntax below:

$ sudo mkdir /etc/notes

This command basically tells Linux to make a *notes* directory, inside the *etc* directory, which is located in *root*. Typing in the full file path will ensure that no matter where you are in the file system, you would be able to create the folder in the right location. That is all you need to do to create a folder or directory in Linux.

Now, to delete files/directories in Linux, you must make use of the command syntax below:

$ sudo rm <folder/file name>

That is *sudo,* a space, followed by the letters *rm*, another space, and then finally the name of the file or folder that you want to delete. As you may have already guessed, *rm* stands for remove. Let us say for example you want to delete a file named *var*. All you need to do is type:

$ sudo rm var

Deleting directories/folders in Linux is a little bit different compared to Windows. In Windows, once you enter the command to delete a folder/directory, it will delete the folder and everything that is inside that folder. In Linux, directory deletion using the aforementioned command will not occur, unless the directory is empty. If a directory contains files, you have to include the *Recursive* argument with the delete command to successfully delete it.

So, how do you do this? Simple. All you need to do is add the -*R* argument at the end of the delete command. Take a look at the command syntax below:

$ sudo rm var -R

The command above basically tells Linux to delete the *var* folder/directory and everything in it. Without the *-R* argument, Linux will not be able to successfully delete a folder that contains files. The only time you would be able to delete a folder successfully without the recursive argument is when the folder is empty to begin with. This is one of the security features that are embedded in Linux, which makes it a truly fantastic operating system.

Let's now talk about renaming files and folders in Linux. Since most people use the Windows operating system, you're probably used to right-clicking a file or folder that you want to rename, choose the *Rename* option, and then type the new name that you want the file or folder to have.

If you're renaming a file or a folder in Windows, you're probably familiar with the Windows command syntax shown below:

C:/ ren <name of original file to rename> <new name of file>

As you may have already guessed, *ren* stands for rename in the Windows system. If, for example, you want to change the name of the file named *alpha* into *beta,* you'll have to type it like:

C:/ ren alpha beta

This basically tells Windows to change the filename from *alpha* to *beta*. Now, let's move over to the Linux operating system. In Linux, there isn't exactly a command that renames a file or folder. What Linux does have is the *move* command.

Let's make use of our previous example. Let's say you want to change the filename of a particular file from *alpha* to *beta*. To do so, you'll have to type the Linux command syntax below:

$ sudo mv <previous filename> <new filename>

So that's *sudo,* followed by the *move* command, which in this case is represented by *mv,* followed by the name of the file that you want to rename, and then followed lastly by the new name you want the file to have. With that syntax in mind, the command to change the filename from *alpha* to *beta* should be:

$ sudo mv alpha beta

As far as Linux is concerned, it is moving the *alpha* file to the name *beta*. It is still technically renaming a file. But in Linux, we use the term *move*. Now, how about moving a file from folder to folder? Well, the same syntax still applies. However, instead of just typing in the name of the files and folders, you must indicate the full path.

For example, let's say you want to move an image file named *image1.jpg* from inside the *var* folder, to the *etc* folder in the *root* directory. To move it, you must type the command syntax below:

$ sudo mv /etc/var/image1.jpg /etc/image1.jpg

That is *sudo,* a space, followed by the letters *mv* for move, another space, the exact file path of the source file, another space, and then lastly followed by the exact file path to the destination. It is as simple as that.

Copying is another important task in Linux. A lot of times, especially if you are dealing with a configuration file, it is essential that you make a backup file before you start messing around with the original file. Because if you mess up the original file, you may end up damaging the program that that file is associated with.

To copy files in Linux, all you have to do is type:

$ sudo cp <name of the file> <name of the copied file>

That is *sudo,* a space, followed by the letters *cp* for copy, another space, the name of the file you want to make a copy of, another space, and then finally the name of the duplicate file. So, let us say you want to make a copy of a file named *file10*. All you need to do is type:

```
$ sudo cp file10 file10.bak
```

Where *file10.bak* is the name of the duplicate file of *file10*. As you can see, it is easy to make copies of files in Linux.

Internet Directories

Basically, the Internet Directories works in such a way that it holds responsibility over sending the right packets, and making sure that they could move across several networks. Its main functions are:

1. **Packet Routing**. This is all about sending packets of data from the destination's source, all the way to where it needs to be used. Unique Protocol Numbers identify these.

2. **Host Identification and Addressing.** With the help of a hierarchical IP System, this one is achieved.

Link Directories

The networking methods are defined within the link layer. The scope is the intervening routers, together with the host network, including the protocols that are being used to describe the topology of the network, and datagrams are also evident with various goals and assumptions together with strict layering. This means that you can implement Linux above any hardware network technology.

With the help of the link layer, packets could easily be moved and could receive driver card packets, and it also means that the layer corresponds to the OSI model.

Directory Lines

Directory 5 to 10

These are used to resolve the host because they work under the syntax *LinuxConnector::resolvehostname()* and they are able to convert IP Addresses and host names with the help of *getaddridinfo()* function. This is way better than just *gethostname()* because it is known as a safe thread.

Directory 13 to 15

These lines are collectively known as *LinuxConnector::resolvehost*. They're able to convert the name string and DNS Host to an IP Address so that every assumption made could be converted to different network addresses.

Directory 16

This is the *socket()* first argument so that you could select specifics and choose protocol families of the communication networks. *SOCK_STREAM* and *PF_INET* should be used as they work well together.

Directory 17 to 20

These are known as *connect::passing()* because it points the user to the right structure with the help of *sockaddr_in* pointers. It will help you know how long the structure is so that you would not confuse it with the other functions of the program and the network itself.

Lines 28 to 34

These make use of the *listen()* function. Basically, you could make TCP Requests and have them queued for you to support participating branches of your network. Some Operating Systems do not support this, though, but then you could just try using the function *m_listening*.

Lines 23 to 27

These are able to bind the listening socket by returning the proper message/bind() values.

Lines 20 to 21

These allow you to listen to the IP and search for connections even abruptly after certain connections end. However, you can disable this by making use of *SO_REUSEADDR* function.

Lines 21 to 32

This gives you in indefinite and continuous number of connections from the clients, and also helps you process a good number of bytes from them, too. It uses the syntax *LinuxAcceptor::start* where you could also process a number of bites from the client. Zero (0) appears when there are no available clients—and servers—around.

Lines 12 to 20

These gives you command-line arguments with the *TCPAcceptor* function. Take note that you do have to specify the IP Address for the server to start making connections.

Lines 5 to 10

These lines will help you realize that the server would start listening to the IP Port and that there would be a command line between the important IP Addresses. Error Messages would be displayed when the user tries to invoke the wrong information.

Lines 13 to 18

With these, you'll know whether the server is listening or not because it uses *m_address*. It also puts and converts bytes into order and prevents socket failures while listening is in order.

Lines 9 to 12

These will help you initialize new sockets in your network by making use of the *PF_INET* protocol. TCP Port will come in order, too.

Line 7

This will help you create the description for the socket so that you could create different calls for different sockets.

Lines 3 to 10

Meanwhile, if you are trying to accept connections from your clients, these lines will come in handy. For these, the *TCPAcceptor::a*ccept syntax is extremely useful. This way, you get all the qualified functions in one thread and you won't get confused.

Encapsulation Directory

Now, in order to provide Linux with its much-needed abstraction layers, Encapsulation is done. It is aligned with the protocol suite's functional division so that each level would be properly encapsulated and dealt with.

Take note that whatever is on top of the layer are those that are closely used in the user applications themselves. However, there is no single architectural model that has to be followed, especially when you have less-defined models such as the OSI model. This is its main difference from other internet protocols, especially the earlier ones.

Conclusion

I hope this book was able to help you master the basics of Linux systems.

The next step is to use Linux in creating your own networks or computer programs.

Finally, if you enjoyed this book, please take the time to share your thoughts and post a positive review on Amazon. It'd be greatly appreciated!

Thank you and good luck!

www.ingramcontent.com/pod-product-compliance
Lightning Source LLC
Chambersburg PA
CBHW071201050326
40689CB00011B/2208